M000200931

# "The Greatest Coach That Never Was"

## Dan Noyes

## Jessica Koob

## Patrick Crowdis

## Kevin Grandin

Published by FastPencil Publishing

"The Greatest Coach That Never Was"

Second Edition

Print edition ISBN: 9781499904314

Copyright © Daniel R. Noyes 2018

http://www.fastpencil.com

Printed in the United States of America

# Table of Contents

This book is the life story of a young man, Patrick Michael Noyes, who was tragically lost in the January 27, 2001, Oklahoma State University plane crash, in Strasburg, Colorado. Ten wonderful men were killed in the crash, changing forever the lives of many people who were relatives, close friends, or anyone with a connection to, or a passion for Oklahoma State University, and in particular for the Oklahoma State Basketball Program. As former Oklahoma State President James Halligan said, " these were all wonderful people, there was not one bad person in the bunch." As President Halligan has pledged, "I will remember always. I will never forget those ten wonderful men." As evidence of his commitment to his pledge, he never leaves home without wearing the orange and black Oklahoma State pin bearing the number "10" in honor of those who perished in the horrible plane crash.

One of those people was Pat Noyes, the son of Daniel R. and Mary V. Payne Noyes. He was only 27 years old at the time of his death, and in all probability had a bright future ahead of him, as an NCAA Division 1 college basketball coach. As you read this book it will show Pat was an individual whom everything he had in his life was due to his drive, desire, and ambition to set goals and to figure out how to achieve those goals. He had set his goal, and he was going to do everything necessary to earn success in the arena he had chosen.

He always spent time meeting people and cultivating relationships, and as a result he was well liked by all. He possessed a charisma which simply made people around him, gravitate to him. This characteristic was sure to help *him get where he was going. Pat had a very unique way of making other people feel important, and he enjoyed doing it. His uncle, Dr. William Makarowski of Erie, Pennsylvania, and Mary's sister Barbara, have a special needs child they nicknamed Muffy. Dr. Bill says " Pat had a special love and affection for Muffy and he treated her with a kindness and empathy that few others ever even considered." He goes on to say "the Patrick we have in our memory bank...a gentleman, through and through who could make those around him laugh and forget about their own problems." He was a special person, a special friend, and a great nephew."*

*Many other people have said Pat was a super human being and friend, he was always there when someone was in need. He reached out to all, and it's what made him special and set him apart from most other people. I hope as you read this book those qualities and attributes of Pat will jump out at you, not just once, but literally time, after time! He made Mary and me proud to be able to say he was our son!!!*

*As a young boy, it was apparent very early he had extreme athletic ability, but he never had the physical size many athletes have. Early on, size didn't matter, as he excelled in both soccer and basketball, while playing with individuals both older and bigger than he was. When he reached high school and college, he played for two good coaches, but they both failed to recognize the "heart" Pat played with, and therefore he never received the amount of playing time he really had earned with his drive, desire, and determination.*

Early in his life, Pat adopted the motto "never give up" for himself, and he never did. He refused to let things bother him, and always looked for ways to better himself, and the people around him, no matter what he was doing. He was a team player in all he did, not just athletics, and he always wanted to help those on his team, to improve.

Pat did not allow his lack of playing time to be an obstacle. He simply did his best at every opportunity he was presented, and as a senior in high school made the play of the game to bring his school the conference championship! His heart, desire and determination made this happen, and he did not allow his size, or lack of size, deter him from doing what he needed to do.

Pat Noyes had the tools to do in life whatever he would have desired to do, but he decided he wanted to coach college basketball at it's highest level. He also targeted his dream job to be head basketball coach at Oklahoma State University, and nothing was going to stop him from achieving his goal. This book will demonstrate how someone with a goal and an extreme work ethic can do anything they set out to do. It took a plane crash to stop Pat Noyes from accomplishing his goal. You will read throughout this book who he was, what he was, what he stood for, and why he was "The Greatest Coach That Never Was."

People who knew him well and understand the game as well as Pat did, were convinced it was only a matter of time, until he reached his goal. Three of those people that had complete confidence Pat would become a great coach were Eddie Sutton, Lefty Driesell, and Roy Williams. These three famous coaches have combined for well over 2000 wins, during their distinguished coaching careers, so *they obviously know a winner when they see one coming along, as they saw Pat. An interesting side bar to this conversation, is the fact Eddie Sutton and Lefty Driesell were the first two division 1 basketball coaches to take four ( 4 ) different schools to the NCAA tournament, and they had one ( 1 ) common assistant between them. The common assistant was Pat Noyes. So Pat was working for, and learning from, two of the winningest coaches of all time! This was a pretty good way to pursue a career of becoming a head division 1 basketball coach. He was well on his way, but unfortunately the plane crash snuffed out all hopes of seeing Pat reach his goal and live his dream.*

*The names used in this book are all factual. They are the names of the people who were Pat's friends, neighbors, relatives and associates who meant so much to him, during his all too short life. In some cases names may be omitted, as a courtesy by the author not to damage an individual's name or integrity. I also want to acknowledge my style of communication has always been "to tell it the way I see it", and I intend to do so in the writing of this book. It's the only way I know, so it is the path I have always followed. Should I damage anyone's feelings by "calling it like I see it" in this book, I apologize in advance and ask that you will understand and appreciate my feelings. Please remember, this book is about the life of Mary's and my departed son, so I may at times become a bit emotional.*

# Dedication

In Loving Memory of Our Beloved Son, Patrick Michael
Noyes
August and September, 2017

It has been nearly 17 years, since we lost Pat, and it has taken me all of this time to muster the courage to write this book. Don't ever buy into the old adage "time heals all wounds." It just doesn't work that way. I have not done a very good job coping with the loss of Pat, but I now believe it is past time for Mary and me to share him, and his incredible all too short legacy, with those who knew and loved him. I hope you will enjoy reading "The Greatest Coach That Never Was."

This book is dedicated to my beautiful, wonderful wife, Mary. Thank you sweetheart, for putting up with me for all these years, and for giving me three of the most wonderful children ever born, one of whom was called home to heaven all too soon.

# Prologue

"A plane has gone down in Colorado tonight. A plane carrying part of the Oklahoma State basketball contingency has crashed shortly after takeoff in a field near Strasburg, Colorado."

Those were the words spoken by a Kansas City newscaster, when we switched on the television to watch the 10 p. m. news on January 27, 2001, after returning home from having dinner with friends earlier in the evening.

Those words began the darkest period of our lives, as for some unknown reason, Mary and I both knew our son Pat was on this plane. There were three small planes carrying the players, coaches, and staff of the Oklahoma State basketball program. The team had played in Colorado Saturday afternoon and was flying home to Stillwater, Oklahoma. It was a flight we have since learned, should never have taken off, as visibility was near zero, due to a heavy snowstorm. Somehow Mary and I both sensed our son was on the fateful flight. We learned ten minutes later in a phone call from our daughter Molly, who was in the Oklahoma State basketball office at the time, and several minutes later in a phone call from coach Eddie Sutton, Pat was on the plane that had crashed and there were no survivors. Pat and nine other wonderful men, most of whom I knew personally, were gone forever.

We had 27 wonderful years with Pat, prior to this night and we will always be thankful for those years, but they just weren't enough. This book is about all those too short 27 years, and why I will always know and believe he was destined to become a truly fabulous college basketball coach. It never came to pass, as God had another plan for Pat. I don't yet understand what God's plan could be, but I'm sure when my time comes and I see Pat again, and I know I will see him again, I will learn and understand God's plan for Pat and the other great men who perished in the fateful flight in January, 2001.

# Chapter 1: The Beginning and the early days

Patrick Michael Noyes was born on July 11, 1973, in Elmira, New York. He was the second son of Daniel and Mary Payne Noyes. Daniel Noyes ll, Pat's brother, was also born in Elmira In January, 1972, so the "Noyes Boys" were less than 18 months apart in age. Mary had always wanted to have a set of twins, and with Dan and Pat, she nearly got her wish. They grew up together and became extremely close brothers, and extremely good friends, sharing many of the same interests in life, particularly basketball.

Pat entered this world in the same manner he departed, very, very, quickly. Mary awoke the morning of July 11, 1973, and said she felt a "whirring sensation", whatever that is. I called the doctor and he said I should bring her to the hospital so he could check how close she was to delivering our second child. My parents came to our house to stay with Dan, while I took Mary to Arnot Ogden Hospital, which was less than three miles from our house. At this point, Mary was not in labor or discomfort, and thought her baby would not be born any time soon.

We arrived at the hospital a few minutes before 8 a. m. I went into the waiting room for expectant fathers, where there were two young men who looked like they had been there literally all night, or maybe even longer, waiting. At 8 a. m. sharp, I started for the pay phone to inform my employer I would probably not be at work that day. Before I even reached the phone, a nurse stepped into the hall and told me if I wanted to see my wife, before she went to the delivery room "you need to come with me now, this baby is here!!!" I saw Mary for not more than a few seconds, and kissed her as the hospital staff was wheeling her toward the delivery room.

Upon returning to the waiting room, the two men looked at me as if to say, "how do you get so lucky and not have to wait for many hours, like we already have???" Within a very few minutes, the doctor appeared and said "congratulations, Mr. Noyes, you have another healthy son." I was absolutely elated with this news and rushed in to see Mary and our new born son.

We had arrived at the hospital shortly before 8 a. m. and Pat's birth certificate states his time of birth was 8:10 a. m. on July 11, 1973. So as previously stated, Pat entered and exited this world in extremely rapid fashion!!! Throughout his 27 years we would learn he did everything this way. When he had an idea in his head and set out to accomplish it, there was no wasting time, he just did it!!!

# Chapter 2: Wellsboro, Pennsylvania

One week prior to Pat's first birthday, we relocated to Wellsboro, Pennsylvania, as the result of me making a job change, which was the first of several job changes I made throughout my career. Wellsboro is a picturesque little town located in the Allegheny Mountains of north central Pennsylvania. It was while we were living in Wellsboro, Dan and Pat's keen interest in sports began to shine through.

Being Wellsboro was a small, but tight knit community, there really weren't a lot of things to do there. High school sports were very important to the local people in north central Pennsylvania, and many people followed and supported their local high school teams. Wellsboro was one of those places where the people were absolutely rabid Wellsboro "Green Hornet" fans.

As young as Dan and Pat were (Dan was just past 2 and Pat was just past 1), we began taking them to every Wellsboro High School sporting event, both home and away. They became very absorbed in football, basketball and baseball, and they very quickly developed an understanding and incredible knowledge in these sports, despite their young ages.

I worked with a man named Dan Denver in Wellsboro, and he and his young family shared with us their love of the high school sports teams in Wellsboro. We became close friends with the Denvers, and our families had a lot in common. Dan and I shared the same first name, we worked for the same company, we both had a son named Daniel and a son named Patrick. Our families went to the same church together in Wellsboro. We also ended up suffering a common tragedy in our lives, after both of our families had relocated from Wellsboro. We both lost our sons, Patrick, at a very young age. Mary's and my hearts go out to both Dan and Pat Denver, as they struggle every day to cope with the death of their son, Patrick. We understand what you are going through Dan and Pat, and believe me, Mary and I are right there with you. May God bless the Denver family.

During our time in Wellsboro, "the Green Hornets" had very good seasons in both football and basketball. The football team had a winning season every year we lived in Wellsboro, and the basketball team, coached by Keith Tombs, won their league championship every season we were in Wellsboro. In particular, I remember one basketball season when the Hornets went 29-3 and advanced deep into the state playoffs, before eventually bowing out.

Looking back at those Wellsboro days, I am certain both Dan and Pat became students of the game of basketball, as they watched and paid close attention to the excellent teams and style of play coach Tomb's teams always played. In effect, Keith Tombs was Dan and Pat's first basketball coach, simply by watching and paying close attention to how his teams played. They both picked up on many of the things those teams did to be successful, and neither Dan or Pat had yet reached age five. They had already become basketball fanatics!!!

There was a park in Wellsboro just a few blocks from where I worked. On nice days I would meet Mary and the boys at the park, where Dan, Pat and I would play basketball for most of my lunch hour. As any good dad would do, I made sure the boys always came out on top. When the boys reached the age and had developed their skills to where they could, and did, beat me regularly in a one on one game, neither of them ever paid me back, by letting me win. They both took pride in "beating me like a drum." Those were the best lunch hours I spent, during my entire career.

We had a very large yard in Wellsboro which served as both a baseball and football field for the neighborhood kids. The Noyes boys and their friends spent many hours playing ball in what became known as "Noyes Stadium", usually beginning in the morning and going on each day, until dusk. Those games were fun for the parents to watch, as all of our boys improved by playing together in those pickup games.

Dan entered kindergarten, while we were living in Wellsboro. Each day, Pat walked to the end of our driveway with Dan, while he waited for the bus to take him to school. Pat always watched as the bus went out of sight, and we could tell by watching him he was anxiously awaiting the day when he too would be going to school.

Sadly, all good things must come to an end, and just prior to Pat's fifth birthday, I accepted a new job in Coudersport, Pennsylvania. It meant that our days in Wellsboro were coming to an end.

Prior to relocating to Coudersport, we spent Pat's fifth birthday at Disney World in Orlando, Florida. Everyone enjoyed the trip. The boys really enjoyed the trip home, when we put our car on the auto train in Sanford, Florida and rode the train to Lorton, Virginia. It was the boys first train trip, and they were completely enthralled by it.

# Chapter 3: Coudersport, Pennsylvania

In July, 1978, we relocated to Coudersport, Pennsylvania. Coudersport was another small, very picturesque community in the mountains of western Pennsylvania. Coudersport was the county seat of Potter County, Pennsylvania, with a population near 2800. Many people claimed there were more deer, than people in Potter County, and it may have been a truism. Nearly every business and school district in northern and north western Pennsylvania, always were closed on the first day of deer season in Pennsylvania, which always occurred on the Monday following Thanksgiving, thus most people in northern and north western Pennsylvania enjoyed a five day Thanksgiving holiday. The first day of deer season in the region very much felt and looked like, a national holiday!!!

In late August of 1978, Pat entered kindergarten, in Coudersport. He went in the afternoon class of Mrs. Moore, a wonderful, experienced teacher whom had been in Coudersport for many years. Pat could not have gotten a better teacher, than Mrs. Moore for his first year in school. Dan entered first grade and had a wonderful teacher in Mrs. Nancy Voorhees.

The boys were able to quickly and happily settle into school in Coudersport. They both had a great teacher, and they made many friends very quickly when school opened in 1978.

Coudersport, like Wellsboro, was very supportive of their high school sports teams. When football season opened in the fall of 1978, the Noyes family became instant Coudersport Falcons fans. As we had done in Wellsboro, we went to every Falcon football game, home and away.

The head football coach in Coudersport was Earl Brown. Coach Brown was about my age, and he and his family lived only two doors from us on Cartee Street. Coach had a son named Doug, who was a year older than Dan. Doug Brown, Dan and Pat became fast friends. The three of them usually went to the varsity football practices and shagged balls for the players. It made them feel like they were a part of the team. It also provided these three young boys with excellent exposure to the game of football, and an opportunity to learn how the game should be played.

In the opening game of the 1978 season, Coudersport played Port Allegheny at home. The game took place on a Saturday afternoon, as at the time there were no lights on the Coudersport football field. Our first game in Coudersport turned out to be a disaster for the hometown Falcons. Port Allegheny handily defeated Coudersport in the first game, 40-0!

Following the embarrassing first game defeat, Coach Brown, his staff, and team mounted a remarkable turnaround, winning the next eight games in succession to finish the season with an 8-1 record and the North Tier League ( NTL ) championship. After losing the first game of the season 40-0, no one would ever have predicted such a remarkable comeback, and much less a championship season for the Falcons, but they did it!!!

Basketball season for the 1978-79 year was a different story for the Falcons, as the team only won three games all season. In the process they suffered many one sided defeats. Despite the team's record we supported them, both home and away, all season long. Don Kirby, who was in his tenth season, was the head basketball coach in Coudersport.

As the next football season began, Coudersport fans were excited about the upcoming season, after winning the league championship the preceding season. Once again, Coudersport opened the season against Port Allegheny, but this time the

Falcons were on the road. Once again, Port Allegheny ran all over the Falcons on opening day, and once again Coach Brown and his staff engineered a second consecutive miracle season, by winning the next eight games, finishing 8-1, and successfully defending the NTL championship!!! Following the season, Coach Brown, who had been coaching at Coudersport for many years, decided it was time for him to step down. He resigned, and his top assistant, Paul Simcoe became the new head football coach, and he held the position for the next 20 years!

Coudersport basketball started off the new season looking much like the previous season, when the Falcons won only three games. Just prior to mid-season the record stood at 5-6, when all of a sudden something happened, and the team took off. The Falcons proceeded to reel off 12 consecutive wins, and stood at 17-6 entering the playoffs. They were also tied for first place in the NTL conference. The Falcons won the first playoff game, but lost the second to NTL rival Emporium. The first playoff game against Emporium was to see which team would advance in the Pennsylvania playoffs. Although the Falcons lost this game, they had a second date with Emporium later in the week for the NTL championship. The championship game turned out to be the best game of the season. In the end, the Falcons prevailed in a tightly contested game throughout, and with the victory came the Falcons first NTL basketball championship since 1964. A drought of 16 seasons had come to an end.

It was in Coudersport, I first began to see both Dan's and Pat's true athletic abilities. There was a traveling baseball team Dan was just old enough to play on. He played third base his first year, and displayed an excellent arm with his across the diamond assists, throwing out many opponents and making very few errors. He also had a booming bat for a player his age.

There were no organized sports for Pat to play in Coudersport, but that did not keep him from playing with older kids, and he was a dynamite player in both pickup football and basketball games. Anyone who watched him could see the potential was definitely there. One day in a pickup football game, Pat fractured a collar bone and declared he would never play football again. This declaration didn't last more than about two weeks, and he was right back out there playing football again, as if nothing had ever happened!

Pat decided one day to take part in an organized either 5K or 10K run in Coudersport. It was for all ages, adults included. Pat had never run in such an event before, and was now going to run in an event with 150 participants of all ages. Bob Chapman, a very good friend of mine, stood with me near the finish line in downtown Coudersport. The race had started outside of town, and would end at the one and only traffic light in Coudersport. Bob and I stood maybe 50 yards from where the runners would come in and finish the race. We were both amazed when all of a sudden Pat rounded the last bend and was sprinting home. He was only six years old at the time, yet he finished sixth in a race with 150 entrants. That day, I realized my son was probably an athlete in the making. Needless to say, I was very excited!!!

Although it was exciting and fun watching the boys begin their actual competitive athletic careers, the most exciting event for us in Coudersport happened on November 10, 1978. On that day Mary and I were blessed with the birth of our daughter, Molly. Molly was the first girl to be born into the Noyes family in 55 years. My dad's sister, Marcia Harasack was 55 years old at the time Molly was born and there had been no other girls born into the Noyes family since then. Needless to say, Molly sat on a very hallowed throne in the Noyes family.

The day Molly was born, I went first to the elementary school to tell Dan that he had a baby sister. Dan was very happy about this. I then went to the house, as Pat was at home in the morning, because he went to afternoon kindergarten. My boss' wife, Betty Hall, was at our house with Pat. When I told Pat he had a baby sister, his reaction was "I don't want a sister, I wanted another brother." I explained to him things don't work that way and we have to accept what the good lord gives us. He bought quickly into this logic and was happy to have his new sister.

Coudersport was a relatively short drive to the Buffalo Bills home in Orchard Park, New York. Mary, the boys and I began going to Rich Stadium, fairly frequently to see NFL football games. Dan and Pat both loved going to those games, and they became avid NFL fans. Dan and I became fans of the Buffalo Bills, which we still are to this day, but Pat for some reason, became a huge Pittsburgh Steelers fan. He was a Steeler fan when he was only five years old, which was before the Steelers had won their first Super Bowl, and he carried his love of the Steelers all the way to his grave. Some of his best friends at the time of his death spoke of Pat, and his "beloved Pittsburgh Steelers!!!" Of course the Steelers went on to win four Super Bowls, and the Bills have never been able to climb to "the top of the hill", although they did eventually advance to the Super Bowl game four consecutive times, only to lose all four of those games, in the early 1990's. Pat took great satisfaction in harassing both Dan and me, because "our Bills" had never won the Super Bowl and his Steelers had won four times. It was a friendly rivalry, but the fact remains, the Steelers were always dominant and the Bills couldn't quite get there. This combination of events always thrilled Pat, and gave him plenty of ammunition to rub it in to Dan and me, and he certainly did it, any chance he got to do so!!!

We had a dentist in Coudersport, Dr. Pete Ryan and his wife, Debbie. Pete was about my age and the Ryan's also had three children, like we did. Pete was a good athlete who had played college basketball at Alfred University with Doug Dowdle. Doug and I had gone through school together and had been basketball teammates in high school. The unfortunate irony of all this was, after we had moved from Coudersport, we learned that Dr. Pete Ryan had lost his son Patrick at about age 30, and Doug and his wife, Anita had lost their son, Christopher at age 21 in a drowning incident in Tennessee.

All three of these tragedies had basically occurred in the same time frame. We have reached out to both the Ryan's and the Dowdle's as we all share the same heartfelt losses in our families. Our hearts also go out daily to Pete and Debbie Ryan and to Doug and Anita Dowdle, as they, like us, must battle through the death of a child. It's not an easy thing for any of us to do, but we have no other choice but to go on living our lives as best we can. It is what it is, and life is not always fair.

In the fall of 1980, I was offered a job in Bradford, Pennsylvania, which I declined to accept. I really was not looking for another job, but was always open to listening, before making a decision. At the time I turned down the offer in Bradford, I really thought that was the end of it and I would not hear anymore about it. Several weeks later, Mary and I were at dinner in Olean, New York, when we happened to meet up with Brad Cooke and his wife at the restaurant. Brad was the man who had offered me the job in Bradford. He told me he had filled the job, but it was not going to work out. He asked again if I might now be interested in the job. I really did not give him any indication of interest, but he called me the next morning at work, which was the day Ronald Reagan was sworn in as president, to ask me exactly what it would take to get me to come to work for him. Rather than just declining again, I gave him my requirements which were much higher than I thought he would go to hire me. Several hours later he called me again and said my request was fine and he and his company, Trico Industries, Inc. were willing to hire me and to meet the conditions I had asked for. Now I knew I was committed and had to accept his offer. While working for Trico, Brad and I became outstanding working partners and friends. Brad Cooke was without a doubt, the best boss I ever worked for. I still think about him very frequently, to this day!

Looking back at the day, I accepted the job at Trico, all these years later, I now recognize God was beginning to put his plan for Pat into place. I would initially be working for Trico in Bradford, Pennsylvnia, but it was Trico who ultimately transferred me to Oklahoma, and this transfer obviously took Pat to Oklahoma, as well. I live many days wondering what would have happened had I not accepted the job with Trico, and remained with Pure Carbon Company in Coudersport, Pennsylvania. I had a good job in Coudersport, we loved the community and life in Coudersport, and we had many friends there. What I didn't see at Pure Carbon was the opportunity for me to advance my career as quickly as I would like. I did see such an opportunity with Trico Industries, and it led me to accept their offer, which ultimately led the Noyes family to Oklahoma. This is very haunting to me as it causes me to wonder had I not gone to work for Trico, and therefore had Pat never ended up in Oklahoma, would he still be here with us today??? That's a question that no one can answer, but in my mind I believe he would still be here. I recognize something else may have happened just as bad as the plane crash, but I don't know that, so therefore I often blame myself for Pat's death, as it was solely my decision to go to work for Trico and ultimately for us to live in Oklahoma. Those thoughts are extremely tough to live with, but again, it is, what it is and we all have to live with the consequences of our actions, so I do every day.

# Chapter 4: Bradford, Pennsylvania

We moved to Bradford, Pennsylvania in early 1981. It would be in Bradford the athletic potential and prowess of both Dan and Pat would begin to really show. Bradford was a community of 12,000 people and had excellent youth sports programs in several

areas. Bradford also had what Molly called "Donalds" (McDonalds ), which all three of our kids saw as a huge plus!

Upon moving to Bradford, both Dan and Pat joined the West Branch Little League organization and became members of the West Branch Yankees. Pat was so thrilled to finally be on an organized team, he wore his baseball uniform to bed the first day he received it. All we could see sticking out from under the covers was the bill on his cap, and he was sound asleep. It was a comical sight! Dan played third base and was selected for the West Branch all-star team his first season. Pat played multiple positions, as he was just learning the game. Both boys looked to be good hitters the first season.

Following the baseball season, New York and Pennsylvania was just developing the NYP ( New York Pennsylvania ) league youth soccer program. The league had teams from Olean, Allegany, Little Valley, Jamestown, Hinsdale, Salamanca and several other small towns in western New York, along with teams from Bradford, Pennsylvania. Teams were by age groups of under 10, under 12, under 14 and 16 and up. Each town had teams in every age group, so there were a good number of teams in the NYP League.

Pat played in the under 10 league his first season, and he immediately became a scoring machine. He scored 16 goals the first year and led his team to an undefeated championship. Dan played on the under 12 team I coached, and was an excellent goalie. In his first season, he allowed very few goals, and our team went all the way to the NYP championship game, where we lost a hard fought battle to Ellicottville, 1-0. It was our only loss all season.

There was a well established CYO basketball league in Bradford. The league was somewhat unbalanced as boys from fourth through eighth grades all played in the same league. Some teams were overstocked with seventh and eighth grade players, while some teams only had fourth, fifth, and sixth grade players. This sometimes gave the teams with predominantly older players a distinct advantage.

I coached a young team in my first season in the league. If memory serves me correctly it was in the winter of 1981. Dan was in fourth grade, so he was able to play, but Pat was only in third grade so he would need to wait a year, before becoming eligible. My first team had a pretty rough season, winning only three games and losing twelve. There was no rule every player on a team had to receive a minimum amount of playing time in each game, but I made such a rule for my team, and said everyone on the team would play at least one quarter every game, regardless of their skill level. It's not fair, in my opinion, to let only a few players get all the playing time, while others who work just as hard at practices, get little if any playing time in games. So everyone on my team got ample playing time, learned much more than if they rarely played, and most importantly, they all had fun. The parents of my players truly appreciated the approach I used in playing all the players on the team. This in itself, was very rewarding to me. I also knew by using this system, my team would get better over the next several seasons.

In the first year, one team finished the season with a 15-0 record, and the league championship. At the league banquet the championship team was awarded the traveling championship trophy, which went every year to the sponsor of the winning team, and then moved on the next season to the sponsor of the new champion. It was explained at the banquet, should a team win the league for three consecutive seasons, the traveling trophy would be retired and remain forever with the sponsor of the team who had won three consecutive championships. The league had been in existence for more than 30 years, and no team had ever managed to retire the first traveling trophy.

As our second season in the Bradford CYO league rolled around, I had pretty much the same players as the first year I coached. The two big differences were the experience my players had gained in their first season, and the second difference was Pat, who was now a fourth grader and was eligible to play in the league, and play he did! In the first game, he became the starting point guard and he completely dominated the game from a defensive standpoint, with many steals and his ability to run the fast break. We won the first game handily, and when the game was over, Joe Vecillio, the head basketball coach at Bradford Central Christian High School stepped up to me and asked, " is the little point guard on your team, your son?" When I said he was my son, Coach Vecillio commented I hope you have no plans to leave town before he's in high school. I already know I want him playing for me someday. Mind you, Pat was only a fourth grader at the time, and had just played his first CYO game, and yet a high school coach already knew he wanted him to play on his team when he reached high school age. This was quite a testimonial to Pat's athletic ability at such a young age. He also was the starting point guard for the Bradford CYO all star team, playing on a team of mostly seventh and eighth graders, while Pat was only a fourth grader! It was totally evident Pat's basketball skill levels were far above most everyone he played with at the time, regardless of age. It was also evident his diminutive size would become a detriment for him in the future. He really needed to grow, and he never did.

We won the CYO championship the first year Pat played, and went on to become repeat champions the next two years, thus retiring the traveling trophy for the first time in league history.

I was so proud of this team! At one point we won 23 consecutive games over a two season span, but we never piled up the score on an opponent. We did play a game when we had a 23-0 lead at halftime, and Pat came up to me all excited and said, "dad we can get a shutout." I told him we do not get shutouts in basketball, but he thought it would be good to do. When it came time to start the second half, I decided not to start Pat, as I knew he would be all over the floor trying to preserve a shutout. When the opponent had scored about 10 points, I told Pat to get back in there. He folded his arms over his chest, and vehemently said "I'm not going in." He was upset with me for not letting him play for a shutout. He never went back into the game. This was a great example of how competitive he was, always!

With Dan and Pat leading the way, my team won the CYO league going away in each of our final two seasons. At the close of Dan's seventh grade season and Pat's sixth grade season, I was transferred to Oklahoma by Trico, and the Noyes domination of the Bradford CYO basketball league came to an abrupt end, after winning three consecutive league championships, and retiring the first traveling trophy for our team sponsor!

Now we go back to the NYP soccer league. In years two, three, and four the Noyes boys participated in the league and played on the same team, with Pat playing the first season up an age level to allow this to happen. I was extremely fortunate to coach a group of young athletes who were good at what they did, understood the word team meant to play together, and they wanted to help each other succeed. As a result, my teams seemed to improve with every game they played, and were successful enough to come away with one third place finish and two league championships in our final three seasons. Pat led the league in scoring every season he played, and amassed 96 goals over his four seasons. Dan was by far and away the best goalie in the league, winning many games by shutout. In our final four league playoff games we won by a composite score of 13-1. Dan allowed but one goal in those four games. It's pretty hard to beat someone when their defense is so stingy. Needless to say, I was extremely proud of, and happy for the basketball and soccer teams I coached in Bradford, Pennsylvania. It was an experience I still look upon today with a great deal of pride, and I will never forget those teams and the players I had the privilege of coaching in Bradford!

Both Dan and Pat played baseball every year we were in Bradford, and they both became reasonably good players. Dan turned into a power hitter who hit many booming home runs . He also became a pretty fair, hard throwing pitcher. Pat was a slick fielding, light hitting second baseman. Pat had such good hand/eye coordination, and a beautiful level swing at the plate, but for some reason he was not a good hitter. I never was able to figure out why he couldn't hit well, as all the right mechanics were there, but they just didn't come together for him. He was an excellent fielding second baseman and he could have played shortstop if he would have had a stronger throwing arm. When we left Bradford, Pat made a decision he would no longer play baseball. His great passion and love for basketball was now showing through big time, and he wanted to concentrate his efforts on the sport. He would do so for the rest of his life, right up until January 27, 2001.

While living in Bradford, Penn State football and the legendary Coach Joe Paterno, became bigger than life to us. We, along with nearly everyone else in Pennsylvania, always knew where Penn State football stood in the national rankings, and we watched Penn State football games on television every weekend. It got to the point everyone was so plugged in to Penn State football, many church pastors gave a report on the Saturday game Penn State had played in the current weekend, before beginning the Sunday church service. It seemed all Pennsylvanians always knew where their beloved "Nittany Lions"stood in the latest college football rankings.

As good a team as Penn State always had, they had never been declared as National Champions, until 1982. In the 1982 Sugar Bowl, the Nittany Lions met Georgia and Herschel Walker in New Orleans, with the winner all but assured to be the National Champion. We had a Sugar Bowl party at our house the night of the game. It was a fun evening, which was made even more fun, when Penn State defeated Georgia to win their first ever National Championship! I can still remember our pastor at church on Sunday morning starting the service by saying, "good morning ladies and gentlemen. It's a beautiful morning in Pennsylvania, and The Nittany Lions Are Number ONE!!!" It brought the house down, and the congregation literally cheered for at least 15 minutes, before the pastor was able to begin the Sunday morning service. It was a fun time to be a Pennsylvanian, and both a Joe Paterno and Nittany Lion fan!!! Joe Paterno, at the time, could have run for Governor of Pennsylvania, and he would have been elected, without a doubt!!!

# Chapter 5: Bartlesville, Oklahoma

Now it was time for our BIG move, all the way from Pennsylvania to Oklahoma. Again, I am not sure if I should ever have accepted the transfer to Okahoma. In fact, I'm sure if I had known then what I know now, we would never have gone to Oklahoma, and it would have kept Pat out of the fateful plane crash. Hind sight as they say is aways 20-20!

Bartlesville, a town of about 35,000 people would turn out to be just a short stop for the Noyes family. When we moved to Bartlesville I had been promoted to general manager of a newly acquired Trico company. It was an excellent opportunity for me at the time, but Bartlesville did not prove out to be a wonderful place for us to live.

Mary began teaching a half day kindergarten class at St. John's School, and Molly was a first grade student at the same school. Dan entered Madisen Junior High School as an 8th grader and Pat was a 7th grader at Madisen. As far as sports programs in Bartlesville, we quickly learned newcomers to town were at a distinct disadvantage. The old town cronies, most of whom worked for Phillips Petroleum, coached many of the youth teams and they wanted the Phillips employees children to get the bulk of the attention and playing time in all the sports programs in town. It was a real battle for newcomers to fit into these programs. In addition, there were only sports teams for eighth graders and no teams for seventh graders at Madisen Junior High School. That meant there were no school teams available for Pat to play for his first year, and he would have to wait a year to play. This obviously did not set well with him.

The boys signed up to tryout for the "classic" or advanced soccer team. I went to watch the tryouts, and it was very evident Dan and Pat were superior players to most of those trying out. But being outsiders, they were both cut from that team, almost immediately. It was a blow to them, but they took it in stride and went to play for teams in the regular Bartlesville City League. They were both standout players in this league, and many people wondered why they were not on the "classic" team. The main thing was that they had fun playing and they completely dominated play in the league. I don't think they learned much, as they were really light years ahead of most of the players they played with or against that season.

When soccer season ended, Dan tried out for the eighth grade basketball team at Madisen Junior High. He made the team, but got very little playing time all season. It was a huge disappointment to him, as not being able to play his first year was to Pat, as there were no seventh grade teams in Bartlesville at the time.

The next basketball season in Bartlesville saw Dan on the freshmen team at Bartlesville Mid High and Pat on the eighth grade team at Madisen. It was evident Dan's game had really slipped, probably from lack of playing time his first year in Bartlesville. I felt bad for him as I watched him struggle on the court all season, and I really thought it would be his last season to play basketball.

One weekday evening in mid December, Madisen played their crosstown rival, Central Junior High of Bartlesville in an eighth grade basketball game, so Pat played in this game. There was no question that Central had the superior team, and should have been able to win the game going away, but it did not happen. Central was totally unprepared for Pat Noyes, as he had not been seeing much playing time, so the Central coaching staff was unaware of Pat and his ability. As usual, Pat did not start the game, but when he came off the bench in the second quarter, with Central leading, Pat took immediate control and Central quickly fell behind and never recovered. Pat began to score and hit his open teammates with passes that led to easy baskets, and all of a sudden, Madisen had a 10 point lead. In the second half Pat continued his excellent play, and Central had no answer. Pat ended the game scoring 17 points and passing for numerous assists, as well as making several steals at key times in the game. Central fought hard in the second half, but this night belonged to Pat, and he was not going to let the game get away. Madisen won that night by about 10 points, and as a result, Pat had won the starting point guard spot for the rest of the season. He was not a big scorer. In fact I think the night he scored 17 points against Central was probably the most he ever scored in a game. Pat prided himself in setting his teammates up for easy baskets, and for playing a hard nosed defense, so it is how he played, and he did it well.

Both boys continued to play soccer on their local teams in Bartlesville, but it was apparent their interest in soccer was rapidly declining, and it was only a matter of time before they stopped playing the game. Dan did continue playing baseball in Bartlesville and was a reasonably good hitter and a fine fielding first baseman who rarely made an error. He would play baseball throughout his entire high school career.

Living in Bartlesville did have the advantage of being only a 45 minute drive to Tulsa, which is a very beautiful and active city. We took advantage of our proximity to Tulsa, by procuring season football and basketball tickets to the University of Tulsa home games. Tulsa was a mid-size Division 1 school, and usually had competitive football and basketball teams. We thoroughly enjoyed going to Tulsa football and basketball games the two seasons we lived in Bartlesville. It was at those games, Molly first began to develop a true interest in sports.

She went to all the games, and was very attentive to what was going on, and she continuously asked her brothers and me questions about what was happening on the field or court. She quickly absorbed both games, and she too was then an avid football and basketball fan. As a result of gaining this exposure to basketball, Molly also began playing the game in our driveway with her brothers. Dan and Pat both seemed to enjoy helping Molly learn to play the game, and it really didn't take long before it was evident she had natural ability for the game, just as Pat did. Dan really never had the natural athletic ability like Pat and Molly did, but he worked extremely hard to make up for his lack of ability. All his hard work eventually paid off, and he became a very good basketball player in both high school and college. Dan's dedication to becoming the best he could be, is really a sterling example of what rewards a great work ethic can produce, not just in athletics, but in life, as well.

We first rented a house in a quiet neighborhood, when we initially moved to Bartlesville. The house had a paved driveway and a basketball goal was mounted in the driveway, so it was right up Pat and Dan's and eventually Molly's alley as well. They began to make friends with some of the other kids who lived around us, and all of a sudden it seemed like there was always a pick up basketball game going on in our driveway. As I said we lived in a quiet neighborhood, but now Pat Noyes lived in this neighborhood, and Pat never played a game quietly. His voice could be heard everywhere when they began playing ball, and it persisted throughout every game. This prompted Mary to say, "Pat you need to quiet down, this is a nice, quiet neighborhood." Pat's very quick witted response to this was an emphatic,"well it's going to change!!!" And change it did, as Pat only knew one way to play, and it was not quiet! The neighbors adapted well to the change, thank goodness.

Such was life in Bartleville, but it soon became time for us to move on to Oklahoma City, the BIG TOWN in Oklahoma.

# Chapter 6: Oklahoma City, Oklahoma

We moved to Oklahoma City in July, 1987, as the result of a merger between Trico and Bakerlift Systems, moving my job to Oklahoma City. The Noyes family had now come full circle from "the sticks" of Wellsboro, Pennsylvania, and now half way across the country to the state capital of Oklahoma, Oklahoma City. The landscape had definitely changed for us. We were also now living in a completely different section of the country, than we were use to. In effect we were strangers and we needed to adapt to our new surroundings. It would be a challenge, but we were confident we could and would, make it happen!

Oklahoma City had something we had never before been able to experience any other place we had lived, professional baseball! Oklahoma City was home to the AAA farm team of the Texas Rangers, the Oklahoma City 89er's. Although Pat had opted to no longer play baseball, he was still a very avid baseball fan and he wanted to go to every game possible. The very first 89er's game we ever went to, Pat was thrilled when he caught a foul ball down the first base line! We kept this ball, until the time of Pat's death and then we gave it to Jason Bell, a good friend of Pat's who pitched at both Oklahoma State and professionally in the minor leagues for several seasons. As a remembrance of Pat, Jason still has this ball today, and says he will keep it forever as every time he picks it up, it makes him fondly remember his buddy, Pat.

In Oklahoma City, Mary quickly secured her first full-time teaching position in many years, She would teach first grade at St. Phillip Neri Catholic School and Molly would also enroll in school there. We had made the decision, upon moving to Oklahoma City we did not want the boys going into any of the large Oklahoma City Public Schools, so we had decided to send them to Catholic School. There were two Catholic high schools in Oklahoma City, Bishop McGuiness and Mount Saint Mary, The Mount as it was usually referred to. Dan and Pat started school at Bishop McGuiness and after two weeks of school it was clear they were very unhappy there. Mary called the principal of "The Mount", explained the situation and asked if she could bring the boys to the Mount for a day of classes to see if would work better for them. The next day, the boys went to Mount Saint Mary High School for the day. They were each assigned a student guide to attend classes with for the day. An announcement was made in the morning that Dan Noyes was a guest at the Mount for the day and would be attending classes with Brian Durow. The announcement went on to say Pat Noyes would be attending classes with Jeff Clark. All students were asked to greet the boys when they saw them in school. When Mary went to pick the boys up at the end of the school day, they were both beaming from ear to ear. They were thrilled with the atmosphere, the students and the teachers at the Mount and they had both decided they wanted to become Mount St. Mary Rockets, and so they did! Their guides for the first day of classes, Brian Durow and Jeff Clark became fast friends, and we are still friends with them today. They have transformed from high school boys to fine young men, and we are proud to call them our friends now, and forever! Brian and Jeff are just two of the great young people Dan and Pat associated with at the Mount, and we are extremely happy they got to spend their high school days with the fine young people at the Mount, and Dan has maintained those relationships all these years.

# Chapter 7: Mount Saint Mary High School

When the boys entered school at the Mount, Dan was beginning his sophomore year, and Pat was a freshman. Their first experience at a Catholic high school was also my first experience with Catholic Education. I had always attended public schools while growing up. Mary on the other hand, had gone all the way through the Catholic school system when she was a student, and now was teaching in a Catholic school, so she knew all about Catholic schools.

I attended a welcome back to school meeting, within the first two weeks the boys started at the Mount. I had never been exposed to a meeting quite like this first meeting. There were a lot of prayers being said, and all of the teachers and staff were talking to the students about love and loving your fellow man. I left the meeting thinking what was discussed during the evening was not "the real world." People don't act this way, and treat each other with the love and respect I observed in this meeting. This somewhat troubled me, as it made me think if the boys were constantly exposed to such exemplary treatment, they would be shocked and unprepared for what happens in "the real world," after they graduated from high school. But then I thought, so what if they get to interact with these wonderful people for four years, and enjoy the kind of life that would come with living the "Mount way." I reasoned it would be good for anyone, so just let it happen. This may have been one of the smartest conclusions I ever came to. Mount Saint

Mary High School, and it's students and teachers turned out to be the finest group of people I was ever associated with. I thank God every day our sons were able to attend Mount Saint Mary High School. It had to have been the best high school experience anyone could have ever had!

As a sophomore, Dan played JV football. This was his first exposure to football, and he seemed to like the game. The football coach knew he had never played, so he made an effort to bring his game along at a slow, but steady pace. Dan picked the game up quickly, and was soon getting quite a bit of playing time. We traveled throughout the state to watch Mount football games, and we quickly found out football was not the Mount's best sport, not even close. It became evident the reason the Mount was not up to speed in football was because the head basketball coach, who was an excellent basketball coach by the way, Skip Ashworth was also the schools's athletic director, and Skip took issue with "his" basketball players playing football. He did not want any of the basketball players to play football and risk injury, therefore he was adamant with both the players and their parents about his basketball players not playing football. The basketball players at the Mount were the biggest and most athletic athletes at the school. Everyone who knows anything about high school sports, knows to be competitive in football, you need to have your best athletes on the field, and because of coach Ashworth's adamant stance about the basketball players not playing football, the Mount never was able to put their biggest and best athletes on the field. As a result, those athletes sat in the stands every Friday night watching the small, lightweight ( 140-155 pound ) football players the Mount did put on the field, getting pounded by much larger and more athletic opponents. This happened night after night, and season after season when I was associated with the Mount, because Skip was in nearly total control of the entire athletic program at the Mount. When Dan and Brian Durow were about to become seniors, they were both making overtures since this would be their last year in high school, they were going to play football. Skip came to Brian's father, Terry Durow and to me and told us both Brian and Dan had no business going out for football for the first time, as seniors, and he solicited our help to make sure it did not happen. Terry and I both let him know right then it was their choice, and we would not interfere if they decided to play football. Skip's influence on them ended up prevailing, and neither Brian nor Dan played football. I still remember Dan on opening night of football season in his senior year, laying on his bed and telling me "dad, I should be playing tonight." That was a long time ago, and he got over it, however the Mount football team did have another dismal season in his senior year. Even though it is my belief Skip was the main reason for the lack of success in Mount Saint Mary football, he is still an excellent athletic director and basketball coach, so I want to give credit, where credit is due, and in this regard Skip Ashworth certainly deserves a lot of credit!!!

Following the football season, Dan and Pat both started their Mount basketball careers. Dan was a member of the JV team the first season, and Pat was on the freshmen team. Pat had still not yet begun to grow very much, and it was now possible his lack of size would stand in his way as a high school basketball player. I always felt the time would come if he did not begin to generate some size, it would affect his athletic career, and now the time was fast approaching.

The JV team at Mount Saint Mary always hosted what was called "The JV Festival" on the Friday and Saturday following Thanksgiving. Dan was on the JV team and would be participating in this event. As stated earlier, I really thought when I saw Dan play the previous year on the Bartlesville Mid High team, it might have been his final basketball season. But when we went to Oklahoma City, and Skip Ashworth first saw Dan play, Skip told me "there's potential in that body, and I'm going to get it out of him."

I will say right now Skip Ashworth was the best high school coach Dan could have had. He absolutely did get the best out of him and helped Dan become the best player he could be. In the first JV festival, it became evident in the first game Skip meant what he said. When Dan first entered the game, he made several foolish mistakes, so Skip pulled him out. In my past experience when this happens, the player rarely gets back in the game. Skip sat Dan down and talked to him a bit, and then to my surprise Dan came off the bench and went back into the game. He played very well, for the rest of the game. I was super impressed with Coach Ashworth for the way he handled Dan in his game. He did not just pull him out and then let him rot on the bench the rest of the game, as many coaches would have done. Rather he showed confidence in Dan, by putting him back into the game encouraging him to play through the problem. Dan did it, and his basketball career at the Mount was off to an excellent start. He had quickly gained the trust of the head coach!

I remember following the first game of the first JV festival at the Mount, I met Coach Ashworth for the first time. I was standing in the lobby of the building that little did I know would someday bear my son's name, when Skip came up and introduced himself. He also thanked me for "bringing two such fine young men to the Mount." He was extremely pleased Dan and Pat were going to school at the Mount. It was a good first meeting between Skip and me.

It was another story for Pat. He struggled to get playing time, as coach Ashworth and the head freshmen coach continuously claimed it was due to his lack of height and physical size. Even though he did lack size it was evident when he did get into a game he was very athletic, much more so than many of the other freshmen who were getting a lot of playing time. Pat refused to be bothered by the lack of playing time, rather he just kept practicing hard every day and trying to improve his game. He also wanted to help his teammates succeed and improve their games. That was Pat. He thought at all times we either all succeed together or no one succeeds, and Pat definitely wanted everyone to succeed, not just himself. He dedicated his entire basketball life to helping his teammates be the best they could be. He just didn't no how to do it any other way, and if he did, he would not accept it. Pat was the epitome of a team player if ever there was one.

Dan and Pat mixed in well with all the Mount students. After basketball games a crowd of Mount students, players and fans alike, would usually go to Denny's Restaurant to get something to eat, commiserate about the game they had just played, and to just hang out and enjoy each other's company. This went on after every game, as I remember. One of the young ladies who was always in this crowd was Carrie Dixon. Carrie was a pretty good athlete who played basketball and softball at the Mount. Carrie was probably as close to a girlfriend as Pat ever had at the Mount. He was much more interested in sports, than girls. But he did hang out with Carrie Dixon, quite a bit. One day he explained to me when he and Carrie went to Denny's after a game he told her she could spend $4.00 on food, and if she spent more than $4.00, she had to pay for whatever she went over Pat's imposed limit. I said, "Pat you can't do that to a girl when you take them someplace." His response was, "dad I have to, do you know how much she can eat?" That again was Pat, the quick-witted one. I bring this up about Carrie Dixon, so I can relate the rest of her story. As I said Carrie was a basketball and softball player in high school. She graduated from the Mount and went on a softball scholarship to Barton Junior College in Kansas. Carrie was a catcher, and one day she took a terrible shot in the shin, while playing softball. The pain was intense and the swelling would not go down. Tests indicated Carrie had bone cancer. They were able to arrest and slow the cancer for a short period of time, but it soon became evident Carrie would be joining Pat in heaven. I remember Carrie asking me at Molly's OSU graduation,"Mr. Noyes, when you pray for Pat, could you please pray for me too." I promised her I would pray for her. I don't recall exactly what year it was, but I do remember sometime during the summer, Carrie Dixon sadly passed away. Six months prior to her passing, she married David Cook, a former high school boyfriend. I hate it such a wonderful young lady is gone, but it also gives me comfort to know Carrie and Pat are forever together in heaven. Carrie Dixon, may you Rest In Peace!!!

During the very first basketball season at the Mount, the boys varsity team had a phenomenal season. Dan even got to dress with the varsity on occasion, and did get some playing time. This team went 29-3 for the season, and went all the way to the state championship game, before losing to Carnegie, 68-67, to finish as runner-up in the state. Losing the state championship by one point was a hard pill to swallow, but as Skip told his team, "don't worry about it, life will go on."

Pat played soccer in the spring season, during his freshmen year. He was a good soccer player, and he eventually played in college, but his high school and college coaches never played him at center forward. They played him at wing, or halfback, so he was never the scorer he had been in the NYP league. Again, it didn't matter to Pat. He just wanted to play and help his teammates improve their games, as well as playing the best he could. So regardless of what position he played, Pat was just happy to be playing.

Dan continued to play baseball. In his sophomore season he played third base, and did well The Mount made it into the State Tournament that year, did very well and all of a sudden they were in the State Championship game. Unbelievable, both the basketball team and now the baseball team had made it to the state championship game, during the same school year. The boys who had been on the basketball team and had lost the state championship by a single point, vowed not to let it happen in baseball. And so it was! The Mount bounced back from the basketball loss and won the baseball state championship for the first time in the history of Mount baseball. What a thrill it was, and what a fitting ending it provided for the 1987-88 sports year at Mount Saint Mary High School. Baseball coach Mike Simon was named Little All City Baseball Coach of the Year, as the headline in the Daily Oklahoman read, "Rocket Baseball Paints the State Blue, We Did It!!!" What a fitting and glorious ending to the school year for a little school like Mount Saint Mary this was! The Mount was the talk of the town as they celebrated their first and only baseball state championship!!!

During the summer months, the Mount played both summer league baseball and basketball. Dan played for both teams every summer. Pat did not play baseball, but he did begin playing summer league basketball with the Mount varsity team. He did well, even though he only got minimal playing time. Even so, Pat kept his head up and continued to work hard and help his teammates, as well as himself. At this point I need to be painfully honest about what I am certain was going on with Pat's lack of playing time. It was true he was small in stature, but he played with more heart and desire than anyone else at the Mount. His hustle and drive provided a benchmark for his teammates they all tried to attain, but most fell short. He was extremely athletic, and was an excellent point guard. If a teammate was open and Pat had the ball, he would always find his open teammate and all of a sudden the open teammate would have the ball and an excellent opportunity to score. On defense, even though he lacked height, he hustled and stole the ball from unsuspecting opponents very frequently.

It seemed to everyone watching Mount basketball, every time Pat entered a game, good things always happened. So why then, was he not playing much more than he was? As I pointed out earlier, Skip Ashworth was the absolute best high school basketball coach Dan could have had. Skip helped Dan to play up to, and at times above his potential, and as a result Dan emerged as an excellent high school player and a fine college basketball player as well. I'm not sure Dan would have been able to accomplish those things, without Skip. When it came to Pat as a player, it was evident to me and many others Skip was not the best coach for him, in fact he held him back from becoming the best he could be. There was a young man on the team who was in the same class in school, as Pat. He was a nice enough young man, but I will keep this polite when I say this particular young man could never, and I mean never, compare to Pat as a basketball player. The problem for Pat, was for some reason Skip was totally enamored with this player, so he played and Pat, sat. This particular player began to get serious minutes of playing time as a sophomore, and was a starter in his junior and senior years. I was never able to figure out why, or what it was Skip saw in this young man, because he just didn't have it, however he sure had the support of the head coach. This was truly a real example of work place politics, taking place in high school sports. I am sure this happens every season and every day, all over America. I will never say Skip Ashworth was not a good basketball coach, because he definitely was a good coach. His won/loss record over many seasons certainly bears this out. I am merely saying Skip was not the best coach for Pat, nothing more.

During Dan's junior and senior years, both the basketball and baseball teams continued to be very successful, and they both made deep runs in the state playoffs both of those seasons, but neither team was able to win another state championship.

In Dan's senior season the basketball team advanced to the state semifinals, before bowing out. Dan probably had the best game he ever played in high school in the semifinal game, but in the end it wasn't enough. The game went into overtime on a night when Dan shot 8 for 9 from the floor, and 9 for 11 from the free throw line to score 25 points. He also grabbed a game high 18 rebounds in the game, but the Mount fell to Carnegie, 69-66 in overtime, and with this loss, Dan's high school basketball career had come to an end. It was a sad night at the Noyes house when this happened, but resilient people don't stay down forever, so we moved on to the other things yet to come.

Dan was the only senior on the baseball team in his final season. The team had another good season, but did not advance as far into the playoffs as was anticipated. With the end of the baseball season, Dan's scholastic sports career had come to an end.

Following baseball season, Dan received two prestigious honors, as well as an opportunity to play in the Little All City basketball all star game. He was first named to the Sooner Conference all conference basketball team. What an accomplishment this was, when I thought back to the days I felt his freshman year would be his final year to play basketball, and now as a senior he had reached the pinnacle in the conference. Dan also received the Mount Saint Mary Christian Athlete of the year award at a banquet in Oklahoma City. Mary and I were extremely proud of our son. Dan was recruited by several small colleges to play college basketball. He ultimately signed a letter of intent to play for coach Roger Trimmell at McPherson College in McPherson, Kansas. This decision certainly turned out to be the best for Dan, as he enjoyed his four years at McPherson College and was successful there both academically and athletically.

Coach Trimmell was much more than just a basketball coach. He was a coach of life. He continuously stressed to his players basketball was just a game, and there are many more important things in life. He stressed the importance of academics and getting a good education. To his credit, every player in coach Trimmell's basketball program who stayed at McPherson College for all four years, graduated. What a phenomenal record this is, as we are talking about a 26 year run, with everyone graduating. This is absolutely incredible! When the Oklahoma City bombing occurred in 1995, Dan was working in Oklahoma City. Within minutes after the bombing took place, Dan's phone rang, and it was coach Trimmell checking to make sure Dan was okay. When he heard about the plane crash, coach Trimmell immediately called Mary and I to express his sorrow and condolences over the loss of Pat. Roger Trimmell was, and is, a very caring and compassionate man. He also traveled the 180 miles from McPherson to Oklahoma City on December 14, 2001, to be present for the dedication of "Pat Noyes Fieldhouse." That's how important Pat was to him! We are very thankful both Dan and Pat were so fortunate to cross paths with him. Thanks coach!!!

At this point, Pat was now a senior at the Mount, and his brother was no longer living at home with us. It was a big change for all of us Mary, Pat, Molly and me. We now needed to learn to live without Dan, and at first it was not an easy task, but we eventually came to deal with it, and things went along just fine.

I became the coach of Molly's 5th and 6th grade basketball team at St. Phillip Neri School. I hadn't coached since Bradford days, so I was really looking forward to this opportunity. When Pat was available he helped me ( if the truth be known, when Pat was available he ran the show, to the delight of the girls on the team). By this time, it was beginning to become evident Pat was destined to be a basketball coach. Coach Ashworth said of all the players he had ever coached, he absolutely thought Pat would make the best coach of all of them. Since Skip had been coaching at the Mount for some 20 years, it was many players he was referring to.

My St. Phillip Neri girl's team had a pretty good season, especially since most of them had never played basketball before.

Molly was now well into the game, had natural athletic ability like Pat, and she began to emerge as the team leader. At the completion of the regular season, we played in the state CYO basketball tournament. We lost our first game to the eventual state champion, knocking us into the loser's bracket where our best possible finish would be 5th place. As we began play in the loser's bracket the girls began to pick up their game as a team. We won our first three games, and knew if we could win the next game, we would get the chance to play for 5th place in the tournament at the Mount Saint Mary Gym. Most of the girls on our team went to the Mount games and they considered the Mount as being home, and they wanted to go "home" for their last game. We won the game, and now we would get our chance to play our final game at the Mount. The girls were thrilled about this, and so was the coach! Our opponent at the Mount was a team from Tulsa. They had a very fast, high scoring guard I thought the best way to defend was to play a box and one, with Molly playing her man to man all over the floor. It worked like a charm, as Molly basically took her completely out of the game, and without their high scoring guard's scoring, we were able to defeat them going away. It was a great win for the St. Phillip Neri Girls as they won the game at the Mount and finished 5th in the state in the CYO tournament. It also marked a successful return to coaching for me.

Mary was offered the principal's job at St. James School in Oklahoma City, which she accepted. She had taught at St. Phillip Neri for four years, and felt it was time for a change. It was also a great opportunity for her to become a principal. Molly was just entering 7th grade at the time and she went with Mary to St. James.

Pat decided he would give up soccer and put all his energy into preparing for his senior basketball season. He trained hard every day of the week and when it came time for school to start, he was in the best shape of his life. One day, Skip remarked to me that he hoped all Pat's hard work and effort would pan out for him in his senior year. Of course we both knew Skip's favorite player was still at the Mount, so for him to make such a remark was not right, as he already knew his favorite player would once again get the bulk of the playing time, while the in shape and better player, Pat, sat and watched this other young man make mistake after mistake, and the young man certainly was not a point guard who was able to handle the ball very well. Pat was all that, and more. For Skip not to play Pat more was not only unfair to Pat, it was also unfair to his entire team, not to have a true point guard on the floor leading the charge in every game.

As his senior season began, it became more evident with every game the Mount needed Pat on the floor much more than he had ever been. He did begin to get some increased playing time, began to score, and recorded assist after assist when he was playing. He did not start any games, but Skip did begin to call upon him when the Mount needed a key basket, or especially when someone full of enthusiasm was needed on the floor to pick the team up. Many times Pat would quickly make a key pass which led to an easy basket, or hit a three point shot immediately upon entering a game. He never let it concern him he was not starting, as he should have been, as he was now getting enough playing time for people to really see how well he could play. Pat still took it upon himself to work with all his teammates to continuously improve their games, as well as his own. It was the way Pat was, he wanted everyone on the team to succeed. This was always his goal every game, to make that happen, and he did. He helped make everyone around him better, and he played to do so every game he ever played.

Looking back, I think the biggest moment of Pat's high school basketball career came near the end of the regular season.

The Mount was playing Tuttle for the Sooner Conference championship. The game was played at Tuttle, as the two teams had already played at the Mount earlier in the season. It was a back and forth tightly contested game throughout either team looked like they could win, or lose, depending on the last minute or two of the game. Pat had been playing between one and two quarters a game, during the second half of the season, but not in this game. I swear Skip had a mental lapse this night and forgot Pat was on the team and was available to play. As the clock wound down toward the final minute of play and Pat had not yet stepped on the floor, it looked like the light finally came on in Skip's head as he looked at the bench, and quickly motioned for Pat to get in the game. Pat popped up off that bench, reported in and waited at the scorers table to be buzzed in. He got on the floor with about 30 seconds remaining, and the Mount trailing Tuttle by a single point. Tuttle had the ball and was trying to run out the clock when Pat stepped between two Tuttle players and intercepted a pass. Skip called his final timeout and all he did in the huddle was look squarely at Pat and said just one word, "score!!!" Jeff Clark threw the inbounds pass to Pat and he drove the length of the court and put up a 10 foot jump shot in the middle of the lane. The ball went over the head of Pat's taller defender, and dropped through the net, giving the Mount an apparent one point lead with less than five seconds remaining. One of the officials was madly blowing his whistle and when the crowd quieted he called off the basket and said Pat had been fouled BEFORE the shot. Because the foul was called as being before the shot, it meant Pat would be on the free throw line to shoot one and one, with the Mount still trailing by one point. With the conference title on the line, Pat calmly stepped to the free throw line and made both halves of the one and one! Tuttle put the ball in play and missed a last second nearly full court shot, and the Mount had won the Sooner Conference championship in Pat's senior season!!! What a great feeling it gave me, and I will never forget as I ran down on the floor to congratulate Pat, all of his teammates were repeatedly chanting, "Pat Noyes, Pat Noyes, Pat Noyes." After all the frustration Pat must have felt over not getting the playing time he truly deserved in high school basketball, it was like justice had been done as Pat had personally delivered the Sooner Conference trophy to the Mount, although he would never say it or see it this way. Basketball to Pat was the ultimate team game. A team won together and they lost together, and no one individual was bigger than the team. It was the philosophy Pat preached to everyone he ever played the game with, and I am sure to him, the Mount, not Pat Noyes, won the conference title in the final regular season game of his high school career!

The Mount advanced into the playoffs in Pat's senior year, as they had done every year our boys were there. The Mount finished the final season Pat played with a 21-5 overall record, but really didn't have much success in the playoffs. They bowed out early, and once again I think a good part of the reason for it was poor point guard play. It did not have to be, had Skip played the right man at the point. But in the end it is what it is, and it didn't happen.

Pat was honored when he was chosen to succeed his brother as the Mount's second consecutive Noyes to receive the Mount's Christian Athlete of the Year award at the conclusion of his senior year. He also received the Mr. Clutch award in basketball for his senior season.

In high school, Pat served as secretary of his junior class and president of his senior class. Mrs. Mary Lee Gill was the faculty advisor for both Pat's junior and senior classes. Mrs. Gill pointed out it was the responsibility of the junior and senior class officers to secure a venue for the school's prom each year. She noted Pat was always the first student to arrive at the Mount when they visited potential prom sites, and he came dressed for business wearing a shirt and tie. Mrs. Gill pointed out "he just naturally knew what to do and how to act and present himself in any situation." She noted that there were many fine students at the Mount, but none came close to matching Pat's know how and skills when it came to such situations, as going out into the public to represent his school. With Pat it just came naturally. He always knew when, and how things needed to be done, and he always did it this way.

Mrs. Gill was also extremely appreciative when Pat nominated her as English Teacher of the Year in both his junior and senior years in high school. Her comment was, "Pat was such a kind and thoughtful young man.

At the end of his junior year in high school, Pat was selected by the Mount faculty to represent the Mount at Boy's State in Miami, Oklahoma at North Eastern Oklahoma Junior College.

Boy's state was held each year, so Pat went there for a full week and proudly represented the Mount, as only he could do with dignity, grace and humility It was the Pat Noyes way!!!

Shortly after Pat had graduated from the Mount, I was offered and accepted an opportunity to become plant manager at Columbian Steel Tank Company in Kansas City, Kansas. Don Wagner, who had been my boss for many years at Trico, had bought Columbian and was taking it private. Don wanted me to come with him to run the plant, which really was a no brainer for me. I jumped at the chance to go back to work for Don. At the time I accepted the job, Mary had just signed another one year contract to continue as principal of St. James School in Oklahoma City. They requested her to give a full school year's notice, before leaving St. James. She felt it necessary to honor this request, which meant that I would be going to Kansas City by myself for nearly a year, before Mary and Molly would be able to join me there. This was not the best arrangement for me, but nonetheless I did it, and was off to Kansas City. Columbian rented an apartment for me to live in, prior to bringing Mary and Molly to Kansas City, and with the very reasonable rates of Southwest Airlines, I was able to fly back on weekends to Oklahoma City.

After graduating from the Mount, Pat decided to join his brother at McPherson College to continue his education. After a one year hiatus the Noyes Boys were together again as roommates at McPherson College.

Pat resumed his soccer career at McPherson College. Mac's soccer program was in its infancy at the time and they needed some experience, so they were pleased to get Pat into the program.

Dan and Pat both played on the JV basketball team, and Dan also dressed for varsity games. Roger Trimmell, who coached at McPherson for 26 years was the head basketball coach at Mac, and his assistant and head JV coach was David Barrett. Dave had come to Mac as a student and basketball player in 1986, and upon graduation had stayed on at Mac in the admissions office and as a part time coach under Coach Trimmell. Coach Trimmell has recently retired, but Dave Barrett is still employed at McPherson College and has now been there for more than 30 years! We have become great friends with both coach Trimmell and Dave Barrett over the years. They are two wonderful people, and we are very pleased to be able to call them both our friends.

Dan played basketball all four years he was at Mac. Although he never reached the heights of his high school days, he was a very valuable cog in the Mac Machine. Coach Trimmell ran a system of changing players every 5 to 10 minutes throughout every game, and Dan fit well into this system. On the average he played about half of every game, as did most of his teammates.

David Barrett still tells the story of a game against Kansas Wesleyan in Pat's freshmen year, when Pat and Dan were playing together on the Mac JV team on a Saturday afternoon. Dave says the game had been a close game, until mid way through the second half when Pat hit a three point shot. The next trip down the floor, Dan hit a three pointer, and the time after that, Pat hit another three. Dave says he will never forget after that third consecutive three pointer, Pat running in front of the Wesleyan bench, and in his best "Dicky V" voice shouting out to the Wesleyan coach "You better get a T.O. Baby!!!" Dave said everyone in the house was able to hear Pat's voice when this happened, and it brought the house down. Dave still thinks about it every time Mac College plays Wesleyan, and it always brings a smile to his face. Another fond remembrance of Pat!!!

Mac was a member of the Kansas Collegiate Athletic Conference ( KCAC ). Although Mac always enjoyed a winning season, they had never been able to win the conference championship to qualify to play in the NAIA national tournament. In Dan's senior season, they came as close to doing it as they ever had. They reached the tournament championship game against Tabor College. The two teams had split their regular season games, and the winner of this last game would move on to the National Tournament in Nampa, Idaho.

Pat had decided at the end of his sophomore year at McPherson, if he wanted to remain in basketball he was not going to be able to do so as a player. His lack of size had caught up to him at the college level, and he realized it would always impact his game. He was certain he would be able to remain in the game, by becoming a coach, and it was the absolute correct decision. He began his journey to become a coach, by first becoming a student manager at OSU He accomplished this by continuously showing up at any OSU open practice sessions he could manage to get to, and by doing so became acquainted with the top two student managers Ron Arthur and Doug Ogle. They made coach Sutton aware of Pat's interest in Oklahoma State basketball, and the rest is history. As he always did, Pat found his way into OSU basketball all by himself. He had no prior connections to the program, but his burning desire to become a part of

OSU basketball was enough to get him started. The plane crash which took his life at age 27, prevented all of us from seeing what a great coach he would have become.

Just prior to halftime of the KCAC championship game at Tabor, Pat walked into the gym. He had gone to practice at OSU, and then borrowed Brooks Thompson's car and made the 160 mile drive, hoping to see "his" Bulldogs win a championship. As things turned out, this was not to be the Bulldogs night. Mac slowly began to self destruct, during the second half, and Tabor turned what had been a one point game at the half into a 20 point rout, and with the win, Tabor was on the way to the National Tournament. What was not lost on us, or anyone else from McPherson was Pat had come 160 miles to see his brother play in his last game ever! It meant the world to Dan, and also to Mary and me. We learned later from Dave Barrett, Pat coming to the game had also made all his former Bulldog teammates happy. Again, this was Pat, always doing whatever it took to make others happy!!!

It was in the same time frame Pat went to Oklahoma State, I left Oklahoma City, for Kansas City. Our family was now living in several locations: I was in Kansas City, Mary and Molly were in Oklahoma City, Pat was in Stillwater, Oklahoma, and Dan was in McPherson, Kansas. It was difficult, but we found a way to make this arrangement work for a year. Molly was in eighth grade when all of this happened, and she was broken hearted, as she had always wanted to follow her brothers to the Mount when it came time for her to go to high school, but now she knew she would be moving to Kansas to go to high school

Mary brought Molly to Kansas on several occasions to visit and eventually choose what school she would attend. I knew this was a hard move for Molly, so I told her she could pick any Catholic school in the Kansas City area that she wanted, and we would buy a house in proximity to the school she picked, and I would commute to work at Columbian, from where Molly had decided to go to school. I felt this was the best I could do for her to soften the blow she would not be going to the Mount. Molly ended up choosing Immaculata ( IMac ) High School in Leavenworth, Kansas. IMac was a smaller, but very similar type school to the Mount. We decided to buy a house in Lansing, Kansas, which was a reasonable 20 mile commute to work for me.

# Chapter 8: Lansing, Kansas

We bought a nice home in Lansing, Kansas. I didn't think we would be there long-term, as we had never lived anywhere for more than five years. I called it wrong, we lived in Lansing for 17 years, until Mary and I had both retired.

Dan had graduated from McPherson College, and had joined the working world. He was working for Tyler Outdoor Advertising in Oklahoma City. The company was run by Tony Tyler, who had graduated from the Mount two years prior to Dan. They joined a men's basketball league in Oklahoma City, so Dan and Tony were once again playing basketball together.

Mary was able to secure a job teaching first grade in Lansing, just a mile from our house. She was happy to be back in the classroom, rather than being an administrator.

Things were falling together for us pretty nicely, in our new locale. The big question would be, how well would Molly adapt to the move, as she had been so focused on following her brothers to the Mount, and now it was not going to happen. She was also farther away from her brothers than she had ever been, and Molly had always depended upon them to help her. She would find out very quickly she would still be able to count on them.

Pat was not running a basketball camp the first week we lived in Lansing, so he was at home. Molly was 14 years old at the time, and found out she was eligible to get a Kansas Drivers license at that age, but only for another week, as the age was changing to 16. She needed to take a drivers test within the next few days, or wait until she was 16. Pat took her out driving at the time, and went over all the scenarios he knew would be on the drivers test. They were out all day and part of the next day, and Pat felt she was ready. They went to the Kansas Drivers Testing Center, and Molly passed the drivers test at age 14! Pat had done it again! He helped Molly learn to drive well in a short time frame, and he was once again her hero! This was just one more feather in Pat's cap.

It would be in her freshmen year at Immaculata High School, Molly's true athleticism was really recognized. Volleyball was a huge sport in Kansas high school athletics, and IMac had an excellent program with Mike Connelly being the head coach. Mike was also the varsity boys basketball coach at IMac. The girls volleyball team had recently won a state championship under Mike, and the boys had not yet won a state title in basketball, but made a deep run in the state tournament, nearly every year.

Molly did not want to play volleyball, but Mike Connelly had seen her participating in his summer camp, and knew she would be a very good volleyball player. Before practice started, Mike recruited Molly, nearly on a daily basis, and he was successful in getting her to go out for volleyball in her freshman year. She played on the JV team, and really played well, but not with much enthusiasm, as she really didn't like or want to play volleyball. I explained to Mike, in Oklahoma, volleyball was really not yet on the map, and told him about all the basketball Molly had played in the Oklahoma CYO league, and how she had gone to every high school basketball game her brothers had played. As a result of all this, she had become somewhat like Pat, and saw basketball as the only sport she truly wanted to play. Mike understood, but he never gave up trying to convince Molly to play volleyball. She only played the first year in high school, and would not play again. I have always thought it was strange, as she enjoyed sports and competition just like both of her brothers.

Basketball was another story! It was Molly's game, and she proved it right out of the box her freshmen year at IMac. The head varsity girls basketball coach at IMac, who was also the boys head soccer coach at the school, was Greg Hohensinner. Greg and his wife Elaine are wonderful people and over the past 20 years we have been great friends with them.

Greg had been the soccer coach at IMac, since the school had begun playing soccer several years prior to us living in Kansas. Soccer was the one sport in Kansas that all schools played at this time in the same classification, for whatever reason. Our first year there, IMac under Greg, had an absolutely phenomenal soccer team. IMac, which was a small school in class 2A in all other sports, made it all the way to the state championship game , in 1993, and were matched against powerful and large St. Thomas Aquinas, a Kansas City area school who's soccer team was ranked in the nation's Top 10, by USA Today. IMac was defeated by Aquinas in the championship game, 4-0, but nonetheless it was a phenomenal effort they had made to go so far, and qualify to play for the state title, against a nationally ranked school.

When basketball started in Molly's freshmen year she began play as the starting point guard on the freshman team. It didn't last long, as about three games into the season, Greg moved her up to the JV team, and then before Christmas break of her freshmen season, Molly was playing on both the IMac JV and varsity basketball teams. The varsity finished the regular season with an 18-2 record, and went on to sweep both the sub state and state tournaments to finish the 1993-94 season as Kansas Class 3A state champions, with a record of 24-2!!!! Molly was the only freshman on the team, and she played in every sub-state and state tournament game on the way to the title. Dan and Pat were absolutely thrilled for their sister. They had both come extremely close to winning a state championship in Oklahoma, but neither one of them had reached the pinnacle, as their sister now had. Dan, who was a senior at McPherson when this happened, was able to see Molly play in all three state tournament games, but Pat was with the Oklahoma State team in Kansas City, as they were playing that week in the Big 8 tournament. Although he was unable to see the Kansas State Tournament, when the "Lady Raiders" took the floor for their first state tournament game, there was a bouquet of flowers on their bench with a card that read: " To Molly and the Lady Raiders, Best of Luck at State, Love, Pat". What a thoughtful gesture this was for Pat to make for both his sister, and the entire IMac team. I often wonder, how many other brothers would have ever thought to do something like that. I don't know the answer to it, but I do know Pat did it!!!

The IMac girls volleyball team, and boys basketball team also made appearances in the 1994 Kansas State tournaments. So IMac had a banner year in sports, during Molly's first year there. That coupled with the winningest season ever in McPherson basketball history ( 21 wins, a record which has since fallen, and now the most wins in a season at Mac is 33! ), made for a very successful sports year in the Noyes house.

The next basketball season saw the Lady Raiders once again in the Kansas State Tournament. They entered the tournament with a 19-3 record, and most IMac fans felt sure the Lady Raiders would capture a second consecutive state championship. It wasn't to be. The Lady Raiders played a very competitive and good game in the state quarterfinal game, but were edged out by a hot shooting Cheyney team. When Dan and Pat called Molly that evening to check on the game results, they were both broken hearted the Lady Raiders season had ended two games short of repeating as state champs. I think both Dan and Pat were every bit, if not more disappointed, than Molly over this loss. They had both expected the Lady Raiders would repeat as State Champions.

With the Lady Raiders out of the state tournament, Mary, Molly, Dan and I were now able to attend the Big 8 Tournament in Kansas City to watch the Oklahoma State Cowboys. Pat would be on the Cowboys bench throughout the tournament, so this would give us a chance to see him, as well. The Cowboys had a 24-10 overall record going into the 1995 Big 8 Tournament, and really had a good chance of finishing high in the tournament. This was both Big Country's ( Bryant Reeves ) and Randy Rutherford's last year at OSU, so the Cowboys wanted to do well, not just for the team, but for those two players who had contributed so much to the Cowboys success over the past four seasons. And do well, they did! The Cowboys won the 1995 Big Eight Tournament, and with the tournament championship came an automatic bid to the 1995 NCAA Tournament. During the 1995 NCAA Tournament, OSU played in one round in Baltimore, on a Friday, and Sunday. After winning the Friday game in Baltimore, coach Sutton took his team to the White House on Saturday to meet President Bill Clinton. President Clinton and coach Sutton had become friends when coach Sutton was the head coach at Arkansas, and President Clinton was the governor of Arkansas at the same time, so the president and coach Sutton were old friends. We have a picture from that White House visit, hanging in our den, of Pat shaking hands with President Clinton in the oval office on St. Patricks Day, 1995. The president is wearing a green tie in the picture to commemorate St.Patricks Day. Mary and I will always treasure this picture of the day Pat met the President of the United States!!!

The Cowboys advanced through the first two rounds of the NCAA Tournament, qualifying for the most prestigious event in college basketball, the NCAA Final Four. OSU drew UCLA in the first round of the final four, at the Kingdome in Seattle. Dave Barrett shares with us another fond remembrance of Pat from the 1995 final four. Dave and coach Trimmell were attending the final four. They went together to see the open public OSU practice session on the floor at the Kingdome. Dave tells us that at the close of the OSU practice, he and coach Trimmell wanted to talk with Pat, so they began to try to draw his attention. Dave says there was Pat "on the biggest stage in college basketball", and when he saw them he smiled from ear to ear and went over to talk with them. Dave noted Pat could have easily given them the cold shoulder and avoided them, but he said "it wasn't who Pat was." He remembered where he came from, and " acted as happy to see us, as we were to see him." Dave remembers that coach Trimmell noted that day after talking with Pat, he wouldn't be surprised at all if one day he and Dave ended up working for Pat on his staff. This is quite a testimonial coming from the coach who had recruited Pat to McPherson College. We'll never get the chance to find out what might have happened, but for all we know, coach Trimmell may have been right!!!

The Cowboys fell short in the final four, losing in the National semifinal game to UCLA. After losing in the final 4, Big Country left OSU and never attended another class. He went home to little Gans, Oklahoma, until he was selected in the first round of the NBA draft by the Vancouver Grizzlies. Country received a $65 million dollar contract when he signed with the Grizzlies. He had a rather short, uneventful NBA career as a back injury cut his career short. He retired from the NBA and went home to Gans to raise cattle.

Following the 1995 Final Four, Coach Sutton asked Pat to accompany him on a trip to Taiwan and the far east on an exhibition trip with a team of Big 8 players to play exhibition games overseas. Pat jumped at the chance, and went with coach Sutton on this trip. While on the trip to the far east, Pat was coaxed into having a drink which contained snake blood. He thus was given the nickname Snake, by some of the OSU players. At the memorial service, following the plane crash, Mike

Noteware, an employee in the OSU Athletics office, referred to Pat as "Snake." Having come from the business world I told him that I did not like that nickname for Pat, because in the business world a snake is a sneak that lurks in the grass and does whatever is necessary to keep others from looking good and advancing up the ladder in their career. Mike's rapid answer to this explanation was, "not that guy, not Pat, he would never do that to anyone." This observation, by Mike Noteware was 100% correct. Pat would never have done anything to harm another person's career. As a side note to this conversation, shortly after the plane crash, Mike Noteware had Pat's name tattooed on his arm.

During the summer of 1995, Pat and coach Sutton attended Big Country's wedding, which actually took place in a pasture near Gans, Oklahoma. Pat and coach Sutton were dressed in suit and tie for the wedding, but Pat told me many of the guests were dressed in jeans and a cowboy shirt. Such was the acceptable way to dress for a wedding in Gans, Oklahoma!!!

During the 1995 final four season, Pat's roommate at OSU was Chad Alexander, who was a freshman basketball player at the school. Pat and Chad became great friends. They worked together on construction jobs in and around Stillwater, throughout the summer and on some weekends, Pat would bring Chad home with him and they went to see the Kansas City Royals play baseball, when they were playing at home. Pat took part in Chad's wedding when he was married, and when Chad was a speaker at the banquet to award the first "Pat Noyes Scholarship" at McPherson College, he actually broke down and cried, during his speech. That's how close he and Pat had become, and Chad was still mourning Pat's death, when he spoke at the scholarship banquet.

Pat served as the head manager in the basketball program, during his final three years he was a student at OSU. At this point in time, Mary and I were becoming very concerned about

Pat's academic standing at OSU, and any time we asked him when he would graduate, he was very evasive. We called Marylyn Middlebrook who was in charge of monitoring academics for all OSU athletes and expressed our concern, about Pat. She agreed to talk with coach Sutton to find out what was going on with Pat's academic progress. What she found was Pat was putting his basketball duties ahead of everything, and was actually treating basketball as if it were his full-time job, with academics being secondary to him. Consequently, anytime an academic course he was taking got in the way of basketball, he merely dropped the course and planned to pick it up later, at his convenience. His GPA was more than satisfactory, but he was short hours toward graduating, as he had dropped several classes too many and had not yet picked any of them back up. Coach Sutton agreed to talk to Pat about this problem. After they talked, Pat got on track, and began making progress toward graduation. Pat told us he knew someone must have talked to coach about him dropping too many classes, because coach had never mentioned this to him before. I told him we had talked to Ms. Middlebrook, who had in turn talked with coach Sutton about it. Pat was not upset with us. He knew it was the right thing to do, and Pat was a man who always prided himself in doing the right thing.

Back at Immaculata, Molly continued her basketball career as the starting point guard during her junior and senior years. She started in 47 consecutive games, during this span, but the team never reached the same heights they had in her first two years. They did however, have winning records in both her junior and senior years. Molly began to receive offers from college coaches wanting her to play for them, after high school. This did not excite her, as basically she had already decided she did not want to play college basketball.

In her final high school season, the Lady Raiders met Wellsville at home, in the first round of the sub-state tournament. Wellsville featured high scoring and very fast, Emily Bloss, whom had already signed a letter of intent to play college ball at NCAA Division ll, Emporia State. Coach Hohensinner decided to employ a box and one defense to try and neutralize Emily Bloss. He rotated with either Paula Winkelbauer or Molly guarding Emily Bloss, throughout the game. This part of the game plan worked well, with Emily Bloss being held 15 points below her scoring average. The problem occurred for IMac, when another Wellsville player emerged and began consistently hitting shots from the right corner. This girl was hitting her shot, nearly every time down the floor in the second half, and coach Hohensinner did nothing to adjust his defense to stop her. Both Steve Rieck and I continuously shouted, "Greg, put somebody out there on her", but it never happened. This young lady was left wide open all game and scored 23 points to lead Wellsville to a seven point win over IMac, ending the Lady Raiders season and Molly's high school sports career. The next day at work, Robert Samsel, whom I worked with at Columbian, and who lived in Wellsville, noted to me "you guys made that gal a scorer last night. That was the first time she ever scored more than seven points in a game." We knew at the time, that Greg needed to change his defense to stop the young lady, but he did not react to it, and this spelled the end of the road for the Lady Raiders. These two teams had entered the sub-state tournament with identical won-loss records, and Wellsville went on to win the state championship, after beating IMac in the first round of sub-state, by only seven points, leaving the IMac faithful with thoughts of "what might have been."

Following her senior season, Molly received offers from several schools to play college basketball. One at a time she said thanks, but no thanks. There were two offers she did consider for a short time, one at Avila University, and the other at then Saint Mary College in Leavenworth. Saint Mary College has since become The University of Saint Mary and competes in the KCAC, with McPherson College, among others. The head women's basketball coach who wanted to recruit Molly was Sandy Mott. She had been watching Molly play all four years at IMac, as well as at her own summer basketball camp at St. Mary College. Sandy Mott even went so far as to promise Molly that she would be the starting point guard at St. Mary in her freshman season. It really doesn't get any better than that, for a freshman recruit, but alas Molly turned the offer down, and decided to remain with her initial decision not to play college basketball. I was somewhat disappointed with her decision, but felt I should not push her to do something she did not apparently want to do, so I kept my mouth shut for once, and let things happen as Molly wanted them to happen. I will say at this point, to this very day I have never understood why Molly did not want to play in college, but at this point in time I really no longer need to understand that.

When Molly graduated from Immaculata High School in 1997, Mary's and my three children had played a combined 33 seasons of basketball! This included youth leagues, CYO, Junior High and High School, as well as Dan and Pat's College basketball. I think watching them play basketball was probably the best time of my life, and I knew when next basketball season rolled around, without a Noyes playing anywhere, I would have some serious withdrawal pains to cope with, and this absolutely did happen to me for some time after Dan, Pat and Molly were no longer playing. I was still unaware the worst ( Pat's death ) was yet to come, and it would really make all other problems and issues inconsequential.

Following high school, Molly entered college at Kansas State for only one year, and then went to Johnson County Community College for her second year, She was slowly easing her way to Oklahoma State, where she really wanted to be.

# Chapter 9: Pat, 1998 Georgia State University

Pat finally made it!!! He graduated from Oklahoma State in 1998, after seven years ( counting McPherson College and Oklahoma State ) in college. We were all in Stillwater to celebrate this gala affair, and it was truly a gala affair. Pat's friends from Oklahoma City and his Mount days, friends from McPherson College, his many friends from Oklahoma State and friends and relatives of ours from back east, all came to Stillwater, Oklahoma, to share Pat's triumphant moment!!! It was a day we were not sure would ever come, but it had finally happened and none of Pat's best friends wanted to miss it, so they did not!!!

I might note at this juncture, the year prior to Pat's OSU graduation, a small Oklahoma high school in the Stillwater area, offered Pat their head boy's basketball coaching job. They had become aware of him and what he did while he was running summer basketball camps at Oklahoma State. The school administration had become very impressed with his coaching ability and style, and wanted him, before any other school district had a chance to hire him. The location was close enough to Stillwater for him to commute and finish his degree. Although he was tempted by the offer, the hangup he had was he would not be able to travel with the OSU team, and he would also miss any home Cowboys games scheduled the same nights his high school team was playing. To Pat, his number one priority was OSU basketball, and that being the case he turned the high school coaching job offer down. This was just another example of people thinking and believing Pat was absolutely destined to be a great coach!

Following graduation from OSU, Pat wanted to go immediately to work for Eddie Sutton on the OSU coaching staff. The problem was coach Sutton's staff was full at the time, and other than remaining as the paid head manager, there was no place for Pat. Coach Sutton put Pat in touch with another legendary coach, Lefty Driesell at Georgia State University. Based on one phone interview and coach Sutton's sterling reference, coach Driesell hired Pat, and without any hesitation he was off to Atlanta. He knew that if he was going to follow his dream and become a head Division 1 basketball coach, he needed to go wherever it took and to put names like Lefty Driesell on his resume. He was now a man on a mission, and he was willing to do whatever was necessary to make his dream a reality. This was for sure an indicator of the success he would achieve, as it absolutely told everyone how driven Pat was to succeed!

Pat arrived in Atlanta, and went immediately to work in the Georgia State men's basketball office as an administrative assistant to coach Driesell. In this capacity Pat was allowed to help coach on the floor at practices, and help on the bench during games, but by NCAA rules he could not recruit in this assignment. It was fine with him. It was a start and Pat knew he could make things happen from there.

Pat and coach Driesell quickly "hit it off" and became good friends. Both of them were avid golfers, so they began to play as much golf together as time permitted them. Coach Driesell and Pat both lived north of Atlanta, so many times Pat would pick coach up in the morning to give him a ride to work. This did not always work out, as Pat liked to get to work much earlier than coach Driesell, and he also liked to work later than coach. This was Pat's extreme work ethic, early to work and then leave nothing undone at the end of the day, no matter how long it may take. It is how Pat always worked! Pat also became a frequent dinner guest at coach and Mrs. Driesell's home.

When coach Driesell accepted the head coaching job at Georgia State he was in his late sixties and knew it would in all probability be his last college coaching job. The Panthers program was in a terrible state of affairs, and coach Driesell had always been a winner, so he was hired to turn the basketball fortunes at Georgia State in the right direction, before he retired. The first item of business to accomplish this turnaround was to bring in a competent staff to help. This staff now included Pat Noyes, among other new faces brought in by coach Driesell.

Pat told me coach Driesell, at age 68, ran the floor with his players nearly every day, and he usually kept up with them. Pat followed in his footsteps and ran the floor with the players everyday. The things coach Driesell and his coaching staff were doing, began to show through, and the Georgia State Panthers began to win. Pat was extremely pleased when he was on the bench the night coach Driesell won the 700th game of his career, while playing Georgia in the Georgia Dome. Mary and I flew to Atlanta to spend a weekend with Pat in January, 1999. We went to a Panthers game and met both coach Driesell and his wife. They were very nice people, and they were both extremely impressed with Pat, which was good to hear. As was par for Pat, he already had legions of friends in the Atlanta area. We met some of them and went out to dinner with them while we visited. Pat was never a stranger for very long, no matter where he went.

We went to a Panthers game on Saturday night and I saw that Pat was just as enthusiastic on the Panther's bench, as he ever was on the Cowboy's bench. At least for the moment, the Georgia State Panthers were his team! Mary and I were flying home on Super Bowl Sunday, but before Pat took us to the airport we went with him to the Georgia State Gym to see him play in an intramural basketball game. What a treat it was! I had forgotten what a good player Pat was, but I soon remembered . He played point guard for his team and was in complete control of the game from beginning to end. He was still the shortest player on the floor, but it didn't matter, he was playing his heart out and leading his team to victory, once again! Following the game he took us to the airport, and as we flew home, Pat went to a Super Bowl Party with friends in Atlanta.

On Mary's spring break from school, and after the final four tournament in early 1999, Mary and I took a driving trip to Savannah, Georgia, a place we had always wanted to see. On our way home, we decided to stop in Atlanta to see Pat. It would be a quick visit, as we had to be home for Mary to return to school on Monday. When we arrived at the basketball office, Pat had just gotten off the phone with coach Sutton. Pat told us coach Sutton had just offered him a job as director of basketball operations, he had already accepted, and would be leaving to go "home" to Stillwater in the morning. He had already informed Coach Driesell he was leaving, and coach said he sure wished Pat would stay with him, but he also completely understood Pat's love for OSU, and knew with this opportunity now right in front of him he would have to go. With that, coach Driesell shook hands with Pat, thanked him for his efforts at Georgia State, wished him good luck and told him he would be watching the papers for news of Pat becoming a head coach, which he said he knew would happen some day soon!

We were only in Atlanta for one night, and the next morning Pat was so excited, he left town, before we did. As far as he was concerned, he was going home!!!

# Chapter 10: Pat's Return To Stillwater and OSU

I always have said Pat had orange ( OSU Orange ) blood flowing in his veins. I sometimes believe I was correct about this. In all my years and many business ventures, I never, and I mean never, saw anyone else have the loyalty to an organization Pat had for Cowboy Basketball. There was absolutely nothing he wouldn't have done for Oklahoma State Basketball to be a complete success. I know he had a fabulous friendship with Sean Sutton, and tremendous respect for Coach Eddie Sutton, as well, but it was his loyalty to his alma mater and it's basketball program which over shattered all else in Pat's mind.

And now he was home in Stiilwater, Oklahoma, Pat's "land of milk and honey." He was in absolute ecstasy to be back at Oklahoma State. He had arrived in time to assume the role of camp director for the 1999 Eddie Sutton Basketball camp, and he jumped in to make the camp the best it could be. Jared Weiberg, who was now a student manager in the OSU basketball program, and would soon be a close friend of Pat's, served as Pat's "right hand man" in directing the camp in his first year as a manager. Jared was anxious to learn from Pat, as he was aware Pat had directed basketball camps for other college coaches in the Big 12 Conference, as well as OSU and Jared wanted to see how Pat handled those camps. Pat was happy to show Jared the ropes and happy to have his help.

Early on, when Pat returned to Oklahoma State, someone high up in the athletic department , and to this day I don't know who it was had selected Pat to be the chauffeur for Mr. T. Boone Pickens, when Mr. Pickens flew into Oklahoma City to go to OSU. Mr. Pickens was a huge OSU donor, particularly to Cowboy football.

The football stadium at OSU is even named "Boone Pickens Stadium." In fact, due to his large donations ( we are told over $165 million ) to OSU, in all essence Mr. Pickens was in charge of the entire OSU athletic program. The point being, Pat acting as Mr. Pickens personal chauffeur from the Oklahoma City airport to Stillwater on Mr. Pickens frequent visits to Stillwater, became very well acquainted with Mr. T. Boone Pickens, and I am certain they had a good relationship, as Pat did with everyone he knew. Later in this book, I will mention why this relationship with Mr. Pickens would have been so important in helping Pat achieve his ultimate goal.

Shortly after his return to OSU, Pat began getting overtures from other schools and coaches who wanted to hire him at a higher rung on the coaching ladder than the rung he currently occupied at Oklahoma State. One by one he politely turned those offers down, as he was committed to being a longtime Cowboy. I am aware of the offers he was receiving at the time, as his sister, Molly, was a student employee in the Oklahoma State basketball office at the time, and she told me about the job rejection letters she had typed and sent out for Pat. I had a tough time understanding Pat's logic of automatically turning down higher level offers than he was at, but yet I knew he had a plan in motion he knew would lead him to reach his goal, and nothing or nobody was going to interfere with this plan!

When Pat returned to Oklahoma State, Sean Sutton had been named as head coach designate, which meant he would be taking over as head coach, whenever his father decided to retire. At this point in time, it looked like a good move for Sean in coach Sutton's eyes, but it really was a trap which would ultimately end Sean's days at OSU. I will reveal more about this, later. The bottom line was while coach Sutton felt he was securing Sean's future in the coaching profession, he was in fact, really destroying it.

Prior to the 1999-2000 basketball season, Pat was to be in a wedding of a member of the OSU basketball staff. The same day as the evening wedding, he had to drive to Tulsa to pick up Andre Williams, a potential OSU recruit. I never knew this story, until I met Andre several years after the OSU plane crash. Andre told me when Pat picked him up he was concerned about getting back to Stillwater in time for the wedding he was to take part in. Pat told Andre to hold on to his hat, as they were going to have to make fast time in the return to Stillwater. Andre said before he knew what was happening, Pat was driving toward Stillwater at speeds exceeding 100 miles per hour, and he ( Andre ) had never been so scared in his life! They didn't get far, before Pat was stopped by an Oklahoma Highway Patrolman. Pat apparently did a good job pleading his case when he told him he was a member of the OSU coaching staff transporting a recruit to Stillwater, and he himself was scheduled to take part in the wedding of an OSU player in less than an hour. Pat offered his cellphone to the patrolman to call coach Sutton to verify his story. The patrolman was apparently chuckling as he bought Pat's story and told them to hurry and get to Stillwater, "but please be careful." Pat thanked the man and continued on to Stillwater, making it just in time for the wedding. This was the first time Andre Williams had ever met Pat, and he says he will never forget this time for the rest of his life.

Andre Williams did end up signing to play basketball at OSU, and he has told me it was due to being hosted by Pat on his recruiting visit, and listening to Pat sell him on all the best reasons for him to come to OSU. Andre said he was seriously considering OSU, before his visit, but meeting Pat sealed the deal for him.

The Cowboys had a great season in 1999-2000, advancing all the way to the Elite 8, before losing to Florida. That Elite 8 game was played in Syracuse, New York. My dad, Pat's grandfather, lived in Elmira, New York at this time, some 100 miles from Syracuse.

The Daily Oklahoman newspaper of Oklahoma City, interviewed Pat and ran a story about his grandfather living close by to Syracuse, and the possibility of him attending the game. Pat was quoted in the paper as saying his grandfather was getting old and he probably wouldn't get many more chances to see him, so he hoped his uncle ( my brother ) would bring his grandfather to the game, which he did. It turned out to be the last time Pat ever saw his grandfather, who lived for another 8 1/2 years, but Pat was gone several years before his grandfather . It's not supposed to happen this way, but it unfortunately did.

With the 1999 -2000 season now in the rearview mirror, Pat went back to his everyday duties in Stillwater. He began making preparations to once again be the camp director of the 2000 Eddie Sutton Basketball Camp, with Jared Weiberg now serving as assistant camp director. Jared's parents, Mick and Vina Weiberg, became somewhat concerned Jared was now buried so deep in the basketball program he was not having "a full college experience." When they asked him about this and said to him " Jared what is it you would really like to do???" Jared's response was he was already doing what he wanted to do, by being with and learning from Pat every day. He also told his parents Pat and he were planning for the future. I know now this was true, and will discuss it further, later in this book. Pat and Jared were on a mission together, and they were going to get it done, no matter what it took. Jared's father, Mick and I were absolutely positive where our sons were headed, but we did not share this information with anyone at the time. Mick and I talked about it, but we agreed it would be best for us to sit back and let their plan play out.

Prior to working solely for Oklahoma State, Pat had traveled around to other colleges, mostly Big 12 Conference schools, and worked summer basketball camps for the coaches at those schools. Doing so obviously helped increase his exposure to other schools and coaches, making those many coaches well aware of who Pat Noyes was, his coaching potential and ability, and the charisma he extended everywhere he went. As was pointed out earlier, Pat was never a stranger for more than five minutes anywhere he went, and this aspect of his character was readily visible at the camps he worked. His coworkers and the participants of all of the camps he worked, always gravitated to Pat, literally within minutes of his appearance on the floor. People were just enthralled by him, and always wanted to share his knowledge of the game, so bringing Pat to their camps was always regarded as a huge plus, by the head coaches of any school able to secure his services for their summer camp. One such coach who valued Pat being at his camp, was coach Norm Stewart, of Missouri. Coach Stewart was not one of Pat's favorite people, as Pat did not appreciate, or approve of coach Stewart's coaching methods when Missouri played Oklahoma State, during the regular season. Coach Stewart, Pat told me, always tried to get into the heads of the opponents by calling out to individual players on the opposing team, various obscenities, as well as insulting the player, and at times, even a player's mother. Pat certainly did not approve of such conduct as this, by any coach. He said that every time Oklahoma State was about to take the floor to play Missouri, coach Sutton would say to his team, "if Norm gets on you don't react to him, just play, and let me and the officials deal with Norm." Then one night at a final four, near Tampa, Florida, Pat went to the hotel dining room for dinner. He was by himself at the time, when he spotted coach Stewart, also by himself. Coach Stewart invited Pat to join him for dinner, and even though he was not thrilled to do so, he accepted and went into the dining room with coach Stewart. Pat said as they dined one on one, Norm Stewart showed the other side of his character, and he proved to be a wonderful person, nothing like the Norm Stewart he knew as a coach on the sideline. Pat came away from dinner with a new and different perspective of coach Stewart. He liked Norm Stewart, the man, but not Norm Stewart, the coach. What he had really wanted to accomplish at the dinner was to establish a favorable relationship with another college coach, and he came away knowing he had successfully done so. This was the way Pat worked, always. Meet someone, talk with them, find out what makes them tick, and then be able to relate to the individual and their likes and experiences. Pat always made the conversation about the other person, never about himself. He had a knack of always making the other person feel important. I think it must be why everyone he met, liked him. I never met anyone, anywhere who knew Pat Noyes, and did not like him. As many people have told me, "to know Pat, was to love him" and most people did just that. He was an incredible young man who people just naturally gravitated to, no matter what the situation. I am extremely proud to be able to say that he was my son!!!

I will always remember the night we were watching the 10 p. m. news on a Kansas City station, and Kansas coach Roy Williams came on the sports news to report Matt Doherty, who was his number one assistant, had accepted the head coaching job at Notre Dame. When asked about his conversation with Matt Doherty, before he had accepted the job, coach Williams said he told him, "Matthew, take the job, because it's a good job and you are ready to step up. Then I want you to call your parents and tell them there will be tickets waiting for them at the airport to fly to Notre Dame tomorrow to see you announced as the new head basketball coach at Notre Dame." Chills went up and down my spine when I heard coach Williams say this, and I said to Mary we would someday be getting a phone call like that, from Pat when he becomes a head coach. I just knew this was going to happen, and I could hardly wait as I anticipated this day I knew would come.

I thought Pat would be able to advance through the coaching ranks, and the assistant chairs more quickly by leaving Oklahoma State for a higher level on the coaching pole, and I also knew he had been turning down some of those offers. I was even told coach Bill Self had made overtures to Pat about joining coach Self on the Illinois staff, where he was coaching , before he moved on to Kansas. I mentioned this to Pat and told him I thought he could accelerate his way to the top by leaving OSU to do so. I pointed out to him when the time was right he would be able to return to OSU. Then I said, "Pat I know what you want, you want to be the head basketball coach at OSU! " He looked at me and responded by saying, "no dad, I WILL be the Head Basketball Coach at OSU!!! " He was so sure of himself when he said it, I am now sure he knew something he was not at liberty to say at the time. I will reveal what I am now sure he knew, before closing this book..

In July, 2000, we had a rare opportunity for our whole family to take a short vacation together. We rented a place on the Lake of the Ozarks, and Mary and I met Molly, Pat, Dan, and Dan's bride to be, Robbie to spend a short week ( 5 days ) at the lake. We had an absolutely fabulous time, and made plans to go back to the lake next summer. It never came to pass.

With the end of summer, came the beginning of the new school year, so Mary returned to teaching in Lansing. Molly had transferred and was now a student at Oklahoma State, as she had always wanted to be. Pat was absolutely delighted Molly had come to OSU.

In September of 2000, Layne Jones, a very close friend of Pat, lost his wife Amy in an automobile accident. Pat had been an usher in their wedding in August, 1996. Layne has told us when he lost Amy, "Pat was there for me like clockwork. Either by phone, text, or in person he was always checking on me. He could not have been any more caring. When I was by myself and really down, Pat would always seem to surface and pick me up, during those dark times."

"I saw Pat the week before the plane crash at Eskimo Joe's. We had a great talk. I had no idea it would be the last time I would see him. When we parted, he gave me a hug, as always, and said "I love ya bro."

"Even though I was taller, I always looked up to Pat. He was always an emotional rock for me."The fact he took time out of his busy schedule, nearly every day to visit me, from September 16, 2000, until his death, speaks volumes about what kind of a man he was. I will never forget him, and I still think about him a lot to this day. I can't wait until my kids are old enough to understand life and it's struggles so I can share Pat's story and his impact on my life with them."

Thanks Layne for sharing this with us, and giving us a great example of what a wonderful person and humanitarian Pat was.

Pat continued working hard for the OSU basketball program, loving every minute of every day, doing exactly what he had always wanted to do. Mary and I were unaware of it, but at this time in his life, Pat had finally developed an interest in a young lady named Stephanie Fisbeck. He had in fact been seeing Stephanie, since the Elite 8 appearance the season before, but had never told us anything about it. Stephanie was a petite, very attractive young lady, and she was a cheerleader at OSU. Pat did not want us to know about this relationship, until he became more sure of where it might be headed. So he did not share anything about Stephanie, with us.

Oklahoma State was scheduled to play Missouri in Stillwater the first Saturday of February, 2001. Mary and I had made plans to attend this game, and it is when Pat had planned to introduce us to Stephanie. The game with Missouri did not happen when it was scheduled, as the plane crash happened first!

January 27, 2001, the Cowboys played Colorado at Colorado. Pat had called us on the phone on Thursday, January 25, to tell us the team was flying on Friday, to Colorado. It would be the last time we ever talked to him. We had always been concerned every time the OSU basketball team played at Colorado. Being a businessman who flew once or twice every month to California for a corporate staff meeting, I knew not to fly anywhere near Denver from the first of September, until the middle of April. There were always large storms in the Denver area, during those times and on occasion a plane would go down there, and many flights were grounded in Denver every year, during those months. The lady at work who made my plane reservations, always knew not to route me anywhere near Denver, at this time of year. So I would not fly commercially into the Denver area, at this time of year, and yet OSU always flew in and out of the same area, every year, with three small planes. Like I said, this concerned Mary and I every year the OSU team went on the Colorado trip. On January 27, 2001, our worst fears came true, and our son, along with nine other great men, lost their lives, because they flew where and when they should not have been flying.

As word of the plane crash and Pat's death began to circulate around our area, our house began filling up with friends coming by to offer their condolences and support. We had friends at our house all night long to help us through this terrible night.

When coach Sutton called us to inform us of Pat's death, he said to me, "Dan, I asked the pilots three times if it was safe enough for us to fly home tonight, and each time they said coach, don't worry about it, we'll be home in an hour and 45 minutes." When I heard this statement by coach Sutton, I nearly jumped through the phone when I said to him: "Coach, if you had to ask the pilots three times if it was safe enough to fly, it must have looked pretty negligible to you, so why didn't you use the common sense God gave you, and wait until tomorrow for better weather!!!" I was absolutely livid with coach Sutton, and it was this statement which made me blame coach Sutton for the crash. I felt this way about coach Sutton for several years, but then I began to do research for this book, and to finally come to my senses. So coach if you are reading this book, please accept my apology for holding you personally responsible for Pat's death. When I first realized Pat was never coming back, I did want someone to blame, and your statement about asking the pilots three times if it was safe enough to fly, made you out to be an easy target. I did not stop to think when you made this statement, you had to be in as much, or more shock as I was, and therefore probably didn't even know or realize what you were saying. I am slow to grasp those kinds of things sometimes, and it took me nearly 17 years to get ahold of myself and analyze what you had to be going through on that terrible night. So I once again apologize to you, and pray you can and will forgive me. I will also say the pain of Pat's death still haunts me every day. I still miss him as much if not more, than ever, and I don't expect to ever get over it. Whenever our entire family has a rare opportunity to be together, there is always a gaping whole we can never fill. This feeling is something anyone who has never lost a child is able to understand I know I couldn't, until we lost Pat. I pray every day no other parents will ever have to go through what Mary and I have had to endure for the past 17 years, but I know it will unfortunately never happen, as parents lose children everyday, Life is not always fair, and losing a child brings this to light very quickly and harshly, believe me, I know.

# Chapter 11: The Memorial Service and Pat's Funeral

Early Monday morning, January 29, 2001, we left for Stillwater to be with Molly and Dan, along with many friends who would be there for Pat and us. This week was the absolute longest week of both Mary's and my life. People from all over the country descended on Stillwater, Oklahoma over the next few days. We saw people we had not seen in years, whom had come to pay their respects to Pat and the other victims of the crash.

Coach Sutton called to tell us that Marty Sargent, an associate A. D. at Oklahoma State would be our contact and representative for the events of the coming week. When we reached Stillwater, we checked into the hotel on the OSU campus where the families of the ten crash victims would be staying. We met Marty and Dan there, and went with them for a meeting with relatives of all of those lost. I can't even remember being in the meeting. The president of OSU at the time was Dr. James Halligan. Dr. Halligan had sent flowers to our room and then he made the rounds to meet all the relatives. Dr. Halligan turned out to be like the "Rock of Gibraltar" for all the victims relatives. It was Dr. Halligan who initiated the phrase "We Will Remember" when referring to those lost in the plane crash, and to this day Dr. Halligan has never left his house without wearing his orange ribbon in honor of those ten wonderful men. Dr. James Halligan, thank you, you certainly have, and will always remember our ten lost Cowboys!!! Dr. Halligan is now retired as president of OSU.

On the Monday evening following the plane crash we were in the lobby of the Holiday Inn in Stillwater when Scott Strellar, Pat's high school JV basketball coach and good friend approached us to say he had someone he wanted us to meet. At this point, Scott introduced us to Stephanie Fisbeck, and told us Pat and Stephanie had established a good relationship together. He told us they ( Scott and his wife along with Pat and Stephanie ) had been planning to attend church together on the Sunday, after the OSU-Colorado basketball game, and then go to Scott's house to watch the Super Bowl game. This plan had obviously fallen by the boards. When he introduced us to Stephanie, Scott told us Pat had been planning to introduce her to us, when we came to the OSU- Missouri game in early February. He decided he would make the introduction for Pat, as he was certain Pat would have wanted him to do. Stephanie was a delightful young lady we liked very much, but we also knew now she and Pat could never be. This thought stung badly. Again, life is not always fair, and Mary and I had now learned this in the most difficult way ever.

The week dragged by slowly, as we greeted long time friends of Pat's and ours throughout the week who had come to Stillwater for the Memorial Service, and to offer their condolences to us for the loss of Pat.

During the first part of the week, none of the men's bodies which had been recovered in Colorado, were yet able to be identified. We were asked where we wanted Pat's body sent when he was identified. We said to send his body to Stillwater, as he considered Stillwater to be his home.

The memorial service was scheduled at Gallagher-Iba Arena for Wednesday, and we scheduled Pat's funeral at a Catholic church in Stillwater, with or without his body, for Thursday, following the memorial service, At the Memorial service, Andre Williams beautifully read "Don't Grieve for me I'm Free'" to the 13,000 people in attendance. A life size picture of each of the "lost Cowboys" was displayed at the front of the arena. Coach Sutton was of course the main speaker at the service. When coach approached the podium it was not difficult to see that he was under extreme pressure and was very fatigued. One by one, coach acknowledged each of the victims, and said something about each one of them. He saved Pat for last, and said "and then there was Pat. He worked harder than anyone on the staff, including me. He opened the office every day and closed it every night. I really don't know what we can do, without him. He simply had the best work ethic of any assistant I ever had, anywhere. He will be missed by all of us." This was truly a very touching tribute to Pat from one of the most successful college baskeball coaches of all time, Eddie Sutton.

There were many college coaches in attendance at the Memorial Service. Head football coaches as well as basketball coaches were in attendance at this solemn event. The one I remember talking to the most was coach Roy Williams of Kansas. Coach Williams was personally acquainted with Pat from the games OSU and Kansas had faced each other as opponents, and from Pat working at several Kansas basketball camps over the years. Coach Williams is a very emotional man, and I could see tears coming down his cheeks as he approached Mary and me. He hugged us and told us how very sorry he was for our loss. He then said that he had always wanted to have Pat on his staff, but he knew it would be next to impossible to get him to ever leave the Cowboys. He was absolutely right in that assessment of Pat, but we certainly appreciated the comments about our son from such a highly regarded and special coach as Roy Williams. Coach Williams also told us if we ever wanted to attend a Kansas basketball game at Allen Fieldhouse, to call his office and tell his secretary we were Pat Noyes' parents and what game we would like to attend. Coach said, the tickets will be waiting for you when you arrive at Allen Fieldhouse. When coach Williams left Kansas and was replaced by coach

Bill Self, coach Self continued this offer of tickets to Mary and me. Coach Roy Williams and Coach Bill Self are two very outstanding and caring men. Thank you to both of these wonderful coaches!

Following the Memorial Service we went to the funeral home to select a casket. I was very, very weak about this process, so I waited outside, while Dan, Mary and Molly did this terrible task. While I was waiting, I received a phone call from Adams County Colorado informing me Pat's body had been identified and would shortly be in transit to the funeral home in Stillwater. That evening we went to the funeral home where Pat's body had been returned. His casket was obviously closed, and there were literally hundreds of flower bouquets in the room. One bouquet which immediately stood out to me was from J.P. Canon Associates and Jim Rohan in New York City. Jim Rohan is a professional employment agent I have never met in person, but over many years I have worked with Jim by phone, as he helped me find and hire employees from all over the country. Jim even helped me to locate several job opportunities, during my career, even though I only ever accepted one job he located for me. I have never met Jim Rohan face to face, but I have corresponded with him by phone for more than 40 years, and I absolutely consider him to be a very good friend. Anyway, Jim had learned of the OSU plane crash through the media, and thought enough of our relationship to send flowers to Pat's funeral. I have continued talking with Jim by phone from time to time, and he is still very hospitable to me even though he knows I am retired and won't be doing any more business with him.

When we had Pat's funeral at a Catholic church in Stillwater, his body was not present at his funeral, as he had not yet been returned to Oklahoma, but nonetheless we went forward with his funeral, as the time and day had been announced and

many guests had arrived to attend Pat's funeral. It was a beautifully conducted mass with a standing room only attendance.

Some of Pat's friends had to stand outside the church and
listen to the event over the intercom system. Tony Tyler, Ty
Tyler, Robert Denegri, and Matt Mollman, all friends of Pat,
Dan and the Noyes family from our Mount Saint Mary Days,
each carried a lighted candle down the aisle to the altar to begin
the mass. Fittingly, we asked Stephanie to do the first reading
at mass and coach Sutton to do the second reading, which they
did. I spoke briefly at the close of the mass and thanked the
hundreds of people for attending Pat's funeral. I was also able
to tell the congregation at this time Pat's body was in transit to
Oklahoma and would be there for his burial the next morning.
Believe me, it was extremely difficult for me to do.

Following the funeral mass for Pat, everyone crossed the
street to the OSU auxiliary gym for a celebration of Pat's life.
The gym was completely packed for the event. Larry Reece, the
public address announcer for both Cowboy football and basketball was the master of ceremonies, and as always he did a superb job. The celebration began with the OSU pep band playing Pat's favorite song, "Ride 'em Cowboy", the OSU fight song.

Several of Pat's very best friends were there to speak to
the audience, about their days and relationship with Pat. I am
ashamed to say I cannot remember everyone who spoke that
day. It has been so long ago, but I am able to relate what some
of those who spoke had to say about Pat.

Chris Choat who had shared a house with Pat for two years
at OSU spoke. He credited Pat for his coming to OSU. He said
when he met Pat and saw his complete enthusiasm for OSU,
there was no place else he wanted to go to school. Chris, who
was engaged at the time of the plane crash, and had asked Pat
to be his best man, told the audience with Pat no longer here
to fulfill this role, there would be no best man in his wedding!
The most touching thing he mentioned was he never saw Pat

any happier "than he was the day his sister, Molly, decided to enroll at OSU."

Scott Strellar, Pat's high school JV basketball coach, spoke and played a tape of a phone conversation with Pat, which actually took place the day of the plane crash. In the tape we heard Pat's voice saying they were going to church, before watching the Super Bowl. Scott felt it was important for everyone present to know Pat was going to church. He closed by recalling a high school basketball game Pat had played in by relating late in the game the Mount had around a 20 point lead, and the ball was rolling toward the sideline, with everyone watching. All of a sudden Pat came flying across the floor and dived head first toward the first row of seats, grabbed the ball and from a prone position on the floor was able to throw the ball backwards to a teammate. When the game ended Scott asked Pat "what in the world were you doing on that last play." Pat answered saying "coach I was trying to get the ball, isn't that the way we're supposed to play???" His point was Pat always did everything full out. It didn't matter to him his team had a 20 point lead with only seconds left on the clock, you always had to give it everything you had. It was the "Pat Noyes way"!!!

The final speaker at the celebration of Pat's life was his brother, Dan.

When Larry introduced Dan he said "watch very closely, because when you see Dan, you will also see Pat. That's how close these guys were." Dan began by saying, " I didn't just lose my brother, I lost my best friend." This statement said it all, until Dan reached the end of his talk. Prior to reaching the climax of his message, Dan inserted a bit of levity into his remembrance of Pat, by relating an incident from a time when Pat had what we should call a semi-serious relationship with a young lady, which in itself was somewhat unusual. It seems the young lady had said to Pat, "if we were married and I was about to have a baby on the same day you had a basketball game, you probably would not even go to the hospital with me, you would go to the game." Pat responded to this by saying no, no no I would go to...wait a minute do you mean just a regular game, or an NCAA Tournament game?" Dan said this answer by Pat, spelled the end of this particular relationship. Once again this was classic Pat, basketball above everything else!!!

Dan concluded his talk by saying, "you wouldn't want me to sing this, but from now on whenever I think of Pat I will be saying to myself " did you ever know that you're my hero, you're everything I ever wanted to be. Now I can fly higher than the eagle, you are the wind beneath my wings." This conclusion brought the house down, and there wasn't a dry eye in the building. What "amazing grace" and class Dan had shown in saluting his brother. When Dan and Robbie were married in April of 2002, the program said, " Best Man: Patrick Noyes, bother of the groom, in loving memory." The spot next to Dan where Pat would have been standing, was left vacant. This was another fabulous gesture by Dan to honor and pay tribute to his brother.

As people began to leave the celebration of Pat's life, we looked toward the rear of the building and we saw the entire Mount Saint Mary basketball team there, all wearing their Mount letter jackets. The team, led by coach Ashworth, moved forward toward Mary and me. Coach Ashworth said they had come to represent the Mount community in paying their respects to their "fallen Rocket." Mary and I were taken back by the fact coach Ashworth had felt it necessary for his entire Rocket team to be there for us, and for Pat. It was then, before the 2001 Rocket basketball team left the building coach Skip Ashworth finally told Mary and me, he had not been fair to Pat, and now realized he should have played him much more then he did, when Pat was a Rocket! He did not apologize, but he did acknowledge he had been wrong. It was good of him to finally acknowledge he had made a mistake in coaching Pat. It was not going to help Pat now, but at least Mary and I now had the satisfaction of knowing coach Ashworth finally realized he had done Pat wrong. As people exited the building, Larry Reece asked the pep band to play Pat's favorite song one more time!!!

The next morning we went to the cemetery for Pat's burial. Again there were many people there, including Sean Sutton, and coach Eddie Sutton to pay their final repects to Pat. Tony Tyler had brought his parish priest from Oklahoma City to officiate at Pat's burial. At the conclusion of the burial we went to Perkins Restaurant for breakfast. Pat and Chad Alexander had helped to build this building, when they worked together on summer jobs in Stillwater.

Mary and I remained with Molly in Stillwater, until the following Tuesday. OSU returned to the basketball court on our last night in Stillwater to play Missouri. It was a big Monday game, and it seemed like everyone in America was rooting for the Cowboys on this night!!! The Cowboys were ready. It was a must win game as far as all the OSU players were concerned. Coach Sutton said he never wanted to win another game more in his life, than he wanted to win the first night back on the court, following the plane crash. And win they did, in dramatic fashion. It was a tightly contested game throughout. It was a game either team could have won. With only seconds remaining on the clock, the Cowboys led by three points and Missouri had the ball out of bounds in the OSU front court. Missouri called time out to set up a play for a three point shot, which would have sent the game into overtime. A Missouri guard drew the task of inbounding the ball. OSU was in a tight man to man defense trying to deny any Mizzou player from getting off a good three point shot. The inbounds pass was deflected by an OSU player and wound up in the hands of one of his teammates. The final horn sounded and the Cowboys had secured a 69-66 victory! Oklahoma State students and fans stormed the court looking like the Cowboys had just won the

National Championship. To the OSU players this win meant even more, than that. They had delivered a win in honor of their fallen OSU brothers, and they felt it "couldn't get any better than that!!! We sat directly behind the OSU bench for the game, and that night I was certain Andre Williams was the best rebounder who ever played the game. In the first half he seemed to grab every rebound there was on the defensive end of the floor. His positioning was so superb no other player, be it a Tiger or a Cowboy, could get anywhere close enough to the ball to contest him for the rebound, and even had they been able to do so, Andre was nearly jumping "out of the gym" on every rebound opportunity. To this day his rebounding efforts that particular night were the very best I have ever seen at any level of basketball, the NBA included. He was a man on a mission, and he was going to make sure the Cowboys won this night.

Finally the next morning, which was a Tuesday, it was time for Mary andme to return home to Lansing, Kansas. All of our friends from Lansing who had been in Oklahoma with us, during our trying time, had gone home, after the celebration of Pat's life.

When we pulled into our driveway in Lansing, we noticed immediately the shrubs in front of our house had all been decorated with Orange and Black OSU ribbons and wreaths, along with cards from many of our friends. We learned Greg and Elaine Hohensinner had coordinated the efforts to get this done for us, and I can't tell you how much it meant to us. But those efforts were not yet over. Several evenings later we went to a basketball game at Immaculata, and when we entered the lobby of the school there was Elaine Hohensinner and several other ladies, passing out orange OSU ribbons to every person who entered the gym. They had a sign reading: "Please wear an orange ribbon tonight in memory and honor of Pat Noyes, brother of 1997 Lady Raider Star and graduate, Molly Noyes."

Every person in the gym, IMac and opponent fans as well, was wearing an orange ribbon, for Pat. And then to top it all off, when coach Hohensinner's Lady Raiders took the floor every player was wearing an orange arm band for their game, also in honor of Pat. Greg and Elaine had again arranged all of this for Mary and I, and we will be forever thankful to them for their friendship and thoughtfulness in our greatest time of need. Coach Hohensinner wore an orange ribbon to every Lady Raider game, for the rest of the season.

While all those things were happening at Immaculata High School, to pay tribute to Pat, something very special was happening in Oklahoma City at the Mount.

The Mount boy's basketball team was enjoying a phenomenal season. The Rockets pulled together and finally won their first-ever State Championship in Basketball. Dan bought shirts for the team to wear, during warmups in the State Tournament which said. "win for Our Fallen Rocket." The Rockets proudly wore those shirts each time they took the floor in the 2001 state tournament. In addition to winning the championship, the championship game had another special meaning. The win was the 300th win for coach Skip Ashworth at the Mount!

Throughout the state tournament, Skip invited Dan to join the team in the pre game locker room talks to talk about Pat, and to convey to the team the importance of winning a state championship and what it would mean to all the Mount alumni players who had come before them, Dan himself included, only to fall short of reaching the top of the hill. The 2001 team would not be denied the state championship!. They won in dramatic fashion. The next day in the paper coach Ashworth was quoted saying "this championship is for Dan and Pat!

# Chapter 12: Post Accident Thoughts and Events

Following the plane crash and Pat's death, I found it nearly impossible to go back to the OSU campus. Our family had enjoyed so many good times on the campus, since 1988, and now I didn't care about ever going there again. I was not happy we had buried Pat in Stillwater, but yet Mary and I both knew it was where he would want to be.

Molly and Stephanie both dropped out of school for the balance of the semester, following Pat's death. Molly was working in either the football or basketball office at the time of the accident, and she was retained in her job after the accident. It kept her in Stillwater to work, and she planned to return to school the next semester. Again neither of these things made me very happy, as I wanted her to get away from Stllwater and OSU forever. Her brother had been killed, due to his involvement with OSU, and at this point in time I was so angry with anyone who had anything to do with OSU, I certainly did not want my only daughter to have anything to do with them, either!

At the time, as I said earlier I held coach Sutton responsible for Pat's death. I no longer feel this way, as I said earlier. I do however, and probably always will hold Oklahoma State University accountable and responsible for the plane crash of January 27, 2001. Why? I myself was a businessman who traveled and flew many, many times for my employer. I have always believed any employer who asks their employees to travel for their job, has a responsibility to make sure the traveling employees reach their destination safely and then return home safely, and it did not happen on January 27, 2001. Someone or someones did not do their job properly that night, and as a result 10 wonderful men are no longer with us. Who made the critical mistake? We do not know for sure, but there are several possibilities. I have always, and still do, question why did the control tower allow that flight to take off that night, when commercial flights out of Denver were being cancelled due to the weather? This in itself makes no sense. If this assumption is correct, how can anyone blame OSU for the crash? That's a pretty easy answer to me. OSU chartered those three small planes for their trip to and from Colorado and the pilots were also hired by OSU. This being the case, someone connected with that flight who ultimately was supposed to be acting in the best interests of OSU, made a very poor decision to allow this

flight, or the other two planes which were a part of the OSU contingency, to go airborne that evening. In addition, an OSU player who was flying on one of the other planes, told me Denver Mills, the pilot of the doomed flight, did not want to fly that night, and he recommended they wait until morning to see if the weather improved. His recommendation, for whatever reason, fell upon deaf ears. I have also been told had Denver Mills been able to see the ground that night, he would have been able to land the plane safely. However, the lack of visibility caused by the falling snow did not allow this to happen. This is just one or two of many possibilities I could site for what happened, but ultimately they all lead back to Oklahoma State, or someone representing Oklahoma State, if only for the evening and this flight. Someone or someones who were in some way connected to Oklahoma State on this evening, failed to do their job correctly, and the rest is history.

Another distinct possibility is the plane which went down was "an accident waiting to happen." I say this as I know one of the victims of the crash, Nate Fleming, told his parents the same plane that crashed was also used by OSU to travel to Texas Tech, the game before the crash and the way the plane was shimmying and shaking, prior to landing, the people on this flight were fearful the plane was going down! Should this be the case, this particular plane should have been grounded, and proper maintenance performed and tested, before it was used again.

I could go on and on and cite other possible causes, but each time those causes lead back to Oklahoma State. Therefore I once again state my premise an employer is always responsible for the safety and well being of any traveling employees. There is no escaping this responsibility for any employer, for any reason.

While sports are an important part of out American culture, an important aspect for us all to learn when something like the OSU plane crash occurs, is sports at any level are really nothing but a game, and there is no game worth anyone's life! I have my favorite teams in all sports, and now when one of them loses, my attitude is "oh well, it's only a game." Think about it, and I believe most of you reading this book will agree with this premise.

# Chapter 13: Pat Noyes Fieldhouse

On December 14, 2001, before a standing room only crowd at Mount Saint Mary Gym, a rededication ceremony took place between the girl's and boy's basketball games against visiting opponent Jones High School. On this night the Mount Gym, which had simply been referred to as the Mount St. Mary Gym, since it's inception 20 years earlier, was rededicated and named forever more, "PAT NOYES FIELDHOUSE." This was the ultimate tribute and honor for Pat, the naming of the gym at his beloved Mount in his name and honor!

There were many speakers that night from the Mount, OSU, and the Sisters of Mercy. They came to talk about Pat, and all he had done for people, and all he meant and would always mean to the Mount. In addition to the speakers other people in attendance included Terry Don Phillips, Athletic Director at OSU, Marty Sargent, Associate Athletic Director at OSU, Roger Trimmell, Head Basketball coach at McPherson College. Patsy Sutton, wife of OSU head basketball coach Eddie Sutton, and Assistant OSU Basketball coaches Sean Sutton and Kyle Keller.

The featured speakers on this evening were two Sisters of Mercy from St. Louis, Mr. Pedro ( Pete ) Cordova, longtime teacher, vice-principal and absolute legend at the Mount, coach Skip Ashworth, Pat's brother, Dan, coach Eddie Sutton, and last but least, Mary and me. The emcee for the evening was Mr. Doug Kretchmar, the principal at Mount Saint Mary High School.

One by one the speakers stepped to the make shift speakers platform which had been set up in the gym. One of the Sisters of Mercy remarked, "for those of you who were fortunate enough to know Pat Noyes, you know he was one tough act to follow." When Mr. Cordova came to the podium he received a standing ovation. Many people who knew him considered Pete Cordova to be the Mount. He had been at the Mount for 20 to 30 years and had won the respect of every student he came in contact with as well as the parents of all the Mount students. He had funny stories about every student, and he called them all by their last name. He always referred to Dan and Pat as "Big Noyes" and "Little Noyes", as he did once again on this night. It was good to hear him call Dan and Pat by those names again, as it brought back so many good memories. Mr. Cordova said " I have always liked this building, except for one thing, it never had a name. Well tonight that is going to be fixed, and when we leave this building in a few hours it will have a wonderful name!" That's the kind of man Pete Cordova was, always saying things to make people feel good.

Coach Ashworth spoke of the sadness he felt when he first learned of Pat's death. He said everyone who knew Pat was better off for having known him. He also talked about the many hours of work he and Pat had done together when Pat had been president of the Mount chapter of the Fellowship of Christian Athletes in both his junior and senior years in high school.

Coach Sutton told the audience Pat had been nearly irreplaceable. He said there were four ( 4 ) people doing the job Pat had done by himself. Pat had worked 14-16 hours a day if that's what it took to get everything done, and coach noted he never once complained about it. He said "to you young parents out there who have a son, Pat Noyes is exactly the person you should want your son to be like. He was the absolute best!"

Dan thanked the Jones team for their patience while this ceremony was going on. He said " I know you came here to play basketball, not listen to speeches, so thanks for your patience." He thanked the Mount administration and board of directors for making it possible to name the gym for his brother. He then concluded by saying "It's a great night to be a Rocket." He was right, it sure was.

At this point Mr. Doug Kretchmar, the Mount principal stepped to the podium and said to the crowd "as principal of Mount Saint Mary High School and with the authority of the board of directors, I hereby proclaim this building forever more to be called " Pat Noyes Fieldhouse!!!" The crowd exploded!!!

Mr. Kretchmar then introduced me and I had the honor of being the first one to ever say, "Good Evening Ladies and Gentlemen, and Welcome to Pat Noyes Fieldhouse!!!" The roar of the crowd was deafening and must have lasted 15 minutes before I could go on speaking. It was a good feeling, because I knew everyone was cheering for Pat. I related to the crowd how I had long been convinced Pat was on his way to becoming a head coach, and before the plane crash I told many people "remember the name Pat Noyes, because someday he is going to take some school to the final four and win the national championship. I pray for two things when that happens, that I will still be alive and that he will get me a ticket!" I did not just make this up for this book. I said it many times to many people, because I absolutely believed it would happen. I still believe today Pat was destined to achieve this, but now we will never have the chance to see him bring his dream to fruition. Once again I say, life is not always fair, and it sure was not on January 27, 2001!!!

The following morning there was a story by Jenni Carlson in the Daily Oklahoman, entitled: "Special gym; special guy; special night."In the article Ms. Carlson quoted Dan saying: "It's always been such a big part of our lives. It's always been a special place. Now it's more so." No matter how much he tasted competition, it was always sweet. He never tired of it", Dan said. Pat's mom, Mary said, " He lived and died for basketball."There was never a sadder truth.

Ms. Carlson wrapped up the article by saying, "Pat Noyes might not have been the best to ever come out of the Mount. But there couldn't have been any better."

And so it was on December 14, 2001, "Pat Noyes Fieldhouse" at Mount Saint Mary High School in Oklahoma City was born. Now Mr. Cordova could finally say "the gym" had a name. Pete Cordova passed away a few short years ago, leaving a hole in the heart of the Mount Community that can never be filled. Even in retirement he always had a tremendous amount of influence over all of us associated with the Mount. His legacy at the Mount will remain forever, as Pete Cordova was the Mount. Thanks Mr. Cordova for all you did for your Mount family, and from my view for all you did for "Little Noyes", and "Big Noyes." May Pete Cordova Rest In Peace." Mr. Cordova's daughter, Talita DeNegri, a 1980 graduate of the Mount, is currently principal at the Mount and is doing a fabulous job. Enrollment at the Mount has nearly doubled, during her tenure, and a large addition to the school is now under construction and is scheduled to open by the beginning of the 2017-2018 school year. Thank you Mrs. DeNegri for all of your accomplishments at the Mount and for what is still to come. I am certain that your dad and Pat are both smiling down at you from above and saying "well done and thank you for helping the Mount be the best it can be!"

The Noyes family will be eternally grateful to the Sisters of Mercy, the Mount Saint Mary Administration and Board of Directors, and the Tyler family who was instrumental in building the Mount gym for their kindness, help and cooperation in dedicating the gymnasium on the Mount Saint Mary Campus, as "Pat Noyes Fieldhouse." May God bless Mount Saint Mary High School, and may God bless Pat!

# Chapter 14: "The Pat Noyes Golf Experience and Scholarship

Two years following Pat's untimely death, Dan along with members of the McPherson College Administration, created and started an annual event at McPherson College in honor and remembrance of Pat. They initiated an annual golf tournament called "The Pat Noyes Golf Experience." The proceeds raised by the annual golf outing go directly into an account at McPherson College for a scholarship in Pat's name. That scholarship is presented each year to a McPherson mens basketball player who most resembles Pat, as both a player, and even more importantly, as a person!

The people who started this event and scholarship are: Pat's brother Dan, Mr. David Barrett of McPherson College, Mr. Michael Schneider, current president of McPherson College, Mr. Eric Vogel, past employee of McPherson College ( Mr. Vogel has since left the employ of McPherson College ), and Mr. Chad Alexander, Pat's former OSU roommate and a current banker in McPherson, Kansas. Thanks to each and every one of you for your herculean efforts to make this annual event and scholarship a reality.

The Pat Noyes Golf Experience and memorabilia auction is held the first weekend of every June, with the proceeds supporting the Pat Noyes Scholarship at McPherson College. The tournament played in June of 2017, was " Pat Noyes Golf Experience" number 14, which ironically was the number on Pat's jersey at Mac College. In January, 2018, Mary and I made the trip to McPherson to present the 11th "Pat Noyes Scholarship." The recipients of this coveted award have been:

1. 2007: Mr. Austin Klumpe.
2. 2008: Mr. Zach Kimble.
3. 2009: Mr. Mark Johnson.
4. 2010: Mr. Marlon Dominique
5. 2011: Mr. Trent Severs.
6. 2012: Mr. Jake Reinhardt.
7. 2013: Mr. Kasey Miller.
8. 2014: Mr. Samson Shivers.
9. 2015: Mr. Derek Bevan.
10. 2016: Mr. Kyle Lakin.
11. 2017: Mr. Ryan O'Hara.
12. Mr. Aaron Bachura

Congratulations to these deserving young men for receiving the "Pat Noyes Scholarship." You are the pioneers of an award which is planned to continue for as long as McPherson College continues.David Barrett has truly become the man who now drives both the golf experience, and the scholarship fund. It is Dave's hope the "Pat Noyes Golf Experience" and scholarship will go on forever at McPherson College. To this end, Dave is preparing his children, Grant and Elle, to be ready to take over the administration of the golf outing and scholarship, when he steps down. He is also asking us to get our four grandchildren involved with Grant and Elle, thus insuring a smooth transition of leadership to carry on this event. I thank Dave for his thoughtfulness and desire to continue to make the "Pat Noyes Golf Experience" the best it can be for years to come.

When I mentioned the memorabilia auction, it is David Barrett who year after year contacts college athletic directors and representatives of professional sports franchises for donations of sports memorabilia from their organizations which are raffled off each year in conjunction with the golf outing, to help sponsor the "Pat Noyes Scholarship." Through the outstanding efforts of David Barrett and the generosity of those organizations contributing items to the annual auction, the endowment fund supporting the "Pat Noyes Scholarship," currently exceeds $100,000, and as a result the amount of the scholarship award is increasing each year. Thank you one and all for whatever you have done to contribute to the continuing success of the "Pat Noyes Scholarship" at McPherson College.

Just prior to the 13th Pat Noyes Golf Experience, in June, 2016, Dave asked me if I would say a few words to the participants. On this day, I did not talk about Pat, or the golf outing, but rather I asked for everyone's prayers for Brooks Thompson. Brooks had played for the Cowboys several seasons ago and was in the NBA four seasons, with the Orlando Magic. He was a good friend of Pat's and now he was lying in a Houston hospital fighting for his life. Less than a week after I had asked for everyone at the golf outing to pray for him, Brooks Thompson passed away at age 45. He had been one of the four people that coach Sutton had brought into OSU to replace Pat, after the plane crash. Brooks had told me at the time he took the job he knew he had "big shoes to fill." Brooks Thompson and Pat are now together in heaven, and I pray Brooks will Rest In Peace.

Many of us who come from out of town for "the Pat Noyes Golf Experience", stay at the Holiday Inn Express in McPherson. Early on a Saturday morning, before the 8 a. m. tee off time, a number of us were having breakfast in the dining area at the hotel and discussing the golf tournament. A lady who was not part of our group, spoke up and asked what we were referring to. One of the golfers explained to her about the "Pat Noyes Golf Experience", and about Pat. All of a sudden the lady broke into tears and said, "Pat Noyes, I knew him." My son went to basketball camp at OSU and insisted that I come to the camp one day to meet one of the coaches at the camp that he thought was the best coach he had ever seen. He introduced me to Pat, and told me "this is the best basketball coach ever" As I watched for a bit, I noticed Pat was all over the floor helping everyone. He did not just pay attention to the better players, he was doing everything he could to encourage and make all the campers feel important and good about themselves. My son was right, he was the best coach I had ever seen, as well!

# Chapter 15: "Pat Noyes Family Locker Room"

When coach Roger Trimmell retired as head coach of the Mac Bulldogs, he was replaced by coach Tim Swartzendruber. Yes that really is coach's last name, it is spelled correctly. I will refer to him as coach Tim, it will be easier that way. Coach Tim came into Mac and jump started the program like a "house on fire." Early on in his tenure at Mac College his team did something the Mac Bulldogs had never done before. It even happened to fall on "Pat Noyes Scholarship Night", making this accomplishment even better. The Bulldogs won the KCAC championship in front of a completely packed house, as they defeated the Bethany Swedes at McPherson. This was a fabulous start at Mac for coach Tim. Everyone at the game reveled in the Bulldogs victory as coach and his players cut down the nets for the first time in school history!!!

This Bulldog team went on to also win the KCAC conference tournament, as well. The NAIA Division 2 National Tournament had moved from Nampa, Idaho to the College of the Ozarks in Point Lookout, Missouri. This location change made a much shorter trip for the Bulldogs. Mac won the first two games of the national tournament and needed only one more win to reach "the final four." All that stood between Mac and an appearance in the final four was the number one team in the nation, Dordt College of Iowa. Dordt led most of the way, but almost miraculously Mac came alive in the last five minutes of the game, and left the number one team in the country in complete disbelief, as Mac defeated Dordt College to move on to the final four. After defeating Dordt, there were no more miracles left in the Bulldog's tank and they bowed gracefully out of the tournament in the national semifinal game. The season was over, but the Bulldogs had set a new team record for wins in a single season as they closed the year with a record of 33-4. Coach Tim used this as an opportunity to campaign to update and refurbish the men's basketball locker room at Mac College. He solicited alumni for the necessary funding. The Noyes family was happy to donate to this cause. Then Dan came up with an idea. He asked coach Tim to name the newly refurbished locker for his brother. Since the completion of this project, the sign on the door reads "Pat Noyes Family Locker Room." Another beautiful tribute to Pat, as well as another reason he will never be forgotten.

# Chapter 16: The Pursuit of a Dream

As we have discussed throughout this book, the goal of Pat Noyes was to become an NCAA Division 1 Head Basketball Coach. Not just any coach, he wanted to be the head coach at Oklahoma State University, and he wanted to be the coach that "kicked in the door" and led the Cowboys to the NCAA championship. I think he was much closer to achieving his goal than we all thought. Everybody but Pat himself. He KNEW where he was headed and when he would get there. With this premise in mind, I ask you to consider what we absolutely knew about Pat, and his drive to become Oklahoma State's head basketball coach and I will also put into the mix a little bit of speculation, which all added together I believe tells us Pat Noyes was near the top of the hill, when tragedy struck on January 27, 2001.

The first statement which really needs to be considered in depth is Pat saying to the author "No dad I WILL be the head basketball coach at Oklahoma State." "I will be," without any doubt in his mind he knew this, and therefore I am certain he knew a lot more than he was able to say when this remark was made. Pat knew completely the landscape of Oklahoma State Athletics and basketball in particular. This being the case I believe he had inside knowledge the Sutton era in OSU basketball was on very precarious ground and was in fact near the end, for both coach Sutton and Sean. Pat would not have done anything to undo the Sutton's, but he would have been willing to take the rebound and run with it, if and when the Sutton tenure was abruptly ended from above, and I believe Pat knew it was going to happen. Why do I believe this? It is a known fact Mr. Pickens was privately chauffeured by Pat between Oklahoma City and Stillwater. It is also known Mr. Pickens was the real Athletic Director at OSU, but had inserted Mike Holder into the position as a figurehead. Make no bones about it, Mike Holder was, and still is, Mr. Pickens hand picked man, and does what Mr. Pickens wants done. In this case, Mr. Pickens wanted the Sutton Era to be over, for whatever the reason. Mr.Pickens and Eddie Sutton were not the best of friends, and as I have been told this had something to do about when Les Miles was hired as OSU football coach. The candidate that Mr. Pickens favored turned the job down, and Mr. Pickens apparently thought it was due to coach Sutton. That immediately built a wall between coach Sutton and Mr. Pickens, which would never come down. Pat knew this. And why did he ( Pat ) all of a sudden become a chauffeur for Mr. Pickens? I have to speculate here Mr. Pickens wanted to discuss the future of Pat and his involvement with OSU basketball. In reality, Mr. Pickens was interviewing Pat, without saying what he was doing. At any rate, we know Pat was not bashful, so we know he would have had his say, with Mr. Pickens.

OSU has always liked to hire alums as head coaches, whenever they can. Pat was an OSU alum through and through. He could have been seen as a Sutton man, which he was to a certain extent. He had a great deal of respect and admiration for coach Sutton. Everyone knew this. BUT he was a Cowboy first and ahead of all else. Pat wanted to be known as a true Oklahoma State man first, and everything else was secondary to him. As was said earlier, "he had ORANGE blood flowing in his veins, Cowboy orange blood!!! Everyone also knew this.

Jared Weiberg told his parents he (Jared )only wanted to hang out with Pat. Why??? Mick Weiberg said to me Pat and Jared were planning, planning their future. I think this probably meant Pat was already assembling "his" staff, and Jared

Weiberg was going to become Pat's number one assistant. This is speculation, but I would not bet against it.

Next are two points I was not aware of, when I began to write this book, but Mary was aware of what was happening and has recently told me of these two important items. Pat was in the process of buying a house in Stillwater. He had already made out a loan application. Think about this for a moment. Was a man who put all his energy, heart and soul into the one dream job he wanted, now going to buy a house to sit long term in a secondary coaching position behind Sean Sutton? He may have been willing to do this very short term, but he knew it would be short term only, and the next step would bring him to the top. Speculation again, but very believable speculation.

I think this next point brings all supposition full circle, and really tells us what was happening behind the scenes. On January 1, 2001, the very month of the plane crash, Oklahoma State increased Pat's salary by 114%!!! Mary knew this, and did not tell me until recently. She saw his first check with the increase applied, so it was not her imagination, it was real. Why was this done and who was behind it being done? It's easy to know why it was done. The powers to be obviously wanted Pat to stay at OSU for a long time. But who was behind such a generous increase? If it was not coach Sutton, which we don't know if it was or not, it had to have been mandated all the way from the top of the Athletic Department, meaning Athletic Director Mike Holder or T. Boone Pickens himself. I won't even speculate on this one. The 114% increase Pat received did not put him near the level paid to a head coach, but it did put him at a level which was sure to hold him, until he did move into the head coaching position.

We also know for sure Pat was turning down coaching offers from other schools, and he had a burning desire to spend his entire career at OSU. He loved OSU with all his heart, and would do anything within legal limits for the school. Simply put as many have said, "Pat Noyes was Oklahoma State Basketball."

If when you, the reader put all of these known facts plus a small bit of my speculation together, it can really only lead us to one logical conclusion, Pat Noyes was within five years or so of reaching his ultimate goal and becoming head basketball coach at OSU. People at the top of the Athletic Department had in all probability already confirmed this to him. All that stood between him and the fruition of his dream was the nearly certain soon to come ending of coach Sutton's tenure, followed by a very short lived head coaching tenure for Sean, and then the door would be open for Pat to do what he had said to me, "dad I WILL be the head basketball coach at Oklahoma State."

"The Greatest Coach that Never was," was about to become "The Greatest Coach That Would Ever be, at Oklahoma State, the moment the Sutton Era came to an abrupt end. The powers to be in the Athletic Department had insured themselves their man was already there and was ready to become the head basketball coach at OSU for the rest of his working career. Pat's dream was nearly complete, but what no one knew at the time was he would not be here to answer the bell when it rang. Once again I say, life is not always fair."

Coach Eddie Sutton was involved in a car accident in February, 2006, and officially retired on May 19, 2006. This opened the door for Sean Sutton to be elevated from head coach designate to head coach.Sean, who officially became head coach at OSU on June 30, 2006, never really had a chance of succeeding in the job. The head people in the Athletic Department wanted the Sutton Era in OSU basketball completely finished. Sean only had the head job for two seasons, and was then pressured by Mike Holder to resign, which he did on April 1, 2008.

I contend at the time Sean resigned, Pat would have been officially named the head basketball coach at Oklahoma State, at the age of 34. Remember his emphatic declaration when he said, "no dad I WILL be the head coach at Oklahoma State!!!" He had been informed from the top of the Athletic Department his time was coming, when the Sutton era ended, and without a doubt it is what would have happened.

Pat would have been highly successful as head coach at OSU, and I am totally convinced he would have remained there for his entire career. It was the job to which he had aspired, and he would have considered it to be his "dream job" to which no other job could ever compare. He would have been a Cowboy for life, and that is how he wanted it!!!

# Chapter 17: Sunrise Beach, Missouri

In 2003, Mary and I bought a small house on the water at the Lake of the Ozarks in central Missouri. We had thought we would like to someday retire on a lake, so we looked at this as a tryout period to see if this was what we really wanted to do, when we retired for good. For the time being, we only planned to spend weekends, vacation time, and holidays at the lake. Our house in Lansing to our house on the lake was only a three hour drive, so our proposed schedule would be able to work well for us.

We discovered rather quickly that we enjoyed the lake life. Molly who had graduated from Oklahoma State, then decided to get additional schooling in physical therapy. She also spent as much time as she could, at the lake, and really enjoyed it. When Molly completed her physical therapy assistant program, she received an internship in a clinic in Laurie, only six miles from our house on the lake. She accepted the internship, and lived full-time in our lake house while in her internship program.

What was happening was definitely positive for all of us, Molly, and Mary and me. Upon completion of her internship, Molly was hired full-time at the clinic she had interned at, and shortly after that, she met her future husband, Trevor Vernon, who lived and still lives today in Eldon, Missouri, 30 minutes from our house on the lake. Mary and I liked Trevor from the very first time we saw him, and when Molly became engaged to him, it made our decision to retire on the lake a very easy one to make.Our house was only 960 square feet, so we made plans to add a 320 square foot addition on the rear of the home to increase the living space to a very livable 1280 square foot retirement home. This has worked out fine for us, and given us a very convenient one story home, right on the water, in which we have now been retired for eight years.

I had decided to leave the pressure packed manufacturing world in early 2003, and was fortunate enough to go to work as Human Resources Director for the Sisters of Charity of Leavenworth in their Mother House, only three miles from our house in Lansing. My commuting days were now history. I would work for the sisters, until I retired in August, 2009.

Mary retired from teaching in June of 2009, and I followed her two months later in August, 2009. By the time we retired, Molly and Trevor had been married for two years, and had their first child, Lilli, and were living in Eldon, Missouri, only 30 minutes from us.

Mary did not like it that Pat was buried in Stillwater, which was more than 300 miles away. We began making plans to move his grave to a cemetery in Laurie, Missouri, only six miles from our house. Trevor had a high school friend who was a funeral director. Her last name escapes me at the moment, but her first name is Suzanne. She agreed to help us have Pat's body, along with the burial items, moved from Oklahoma to Laurie , Missouri and reburied in the cemetery at her funeral home. This procedure, with all the different laws of both states, took nearly a full year to accomplish. Suzanne followed through, until she was successful in completing the arrangements, and in July, 2010, we had Pat's grave relocated to Laurie, Missouri. I still have a very difficult time going there, but Mary does go to the cemetery about once a week to check on the condition of his grave and to pray for Pat. I am happy for her we did this, as it is comforting to Mary having Pat's grave so near where we live. We had him first buried in Stillwater, because we knew it was where he had considered home, but he was there for nine years and over this time span, most of the people he was best acquainted with in Stillwater have moved on. So we felt it was the right time to bring his grave to where we live, and so that transpired.

# Chapter 18: Lake West Christian Academy

There was a small christian school in Sunrise Beach, Missouri called Lake West Christian Academy. The school was founded sometime around the year 2000, by Pastor Nick Stutesman, the pastor of Sunrise Bible Church in Sunrise Beach.

The first year (2009) we had lived in Sunrise Beach, people in town had learned about Pat, who he had been, and what his goal for his life's work was. Along with that they had found out that I had successfully coached basketball and soccer in New York, Pennsylvania and Oklahoma. These people began talking to me about Lake West Christian Academy and telling me it was a good school, but if it would never be able to grow, without an athletic program. The school was pre-k thru 12 school, but after grades 6 and 7, I was told many students dropped out and went to public schools, because there was no sports programs at the school for them to participate in, so they would transfer to a public school that had interscholastic athletic teams for them to be a part of. These people continuously urged me to go see Pastor Nick Stutesman to see if I might be able to help Lake West Christian Academy in an effort to develop an athletic program at the school.

I made an appointment to visit with Pastor Nick, and found him to be a very nice, down to earth man. I related to him how many people in and around the area of the school had asked me to see him about the lack of any interscholastic sports programs being available at his school. He agreed with this and asked me what I had in mind. I jumped in and said that I would be happy to come to Lake West Christian Academy to be voluntary athletic director and do my best to get a program going for him. Pastor's only response to my proposal was, "when can you start? Do we have enough time to still have a basketball camp this summer ?" Since school would be starting in less than a month, I told him we would be cutting it close, but if it was what he wanted I would try to make it happen. That day, the Athletic and interscholastic sports programs were born at Lake West Christian Academy ( LWCA ).

We somehow managed to have a small basketball camp the first summer, with 15-18 participants, but nonetheless, it was a start. Over the next four years the participation level would increase to 85 students, and our camp became known as the best basketball camp in the entire lake area. It happened as a result of my efforts to bring to our camp former Division I basketball players, NAIA coaches, NCAA Division 3 coaches, and players from both NAIA schools, and D3 schools. Coach Greg Hohensinner, previous head coach of the Immaculata Lady Raiders, was now the coach at the new St. James Academy in Lenexa, Kansas, and he joined me for the entire week of our first camp. Greg absolutely taught me how to properly run a basketball camp, and I will always be grateful to him for this.

Andre Williams and Joe Adkins, both former Oklahoma State players were frequent guests all four years of our camp, along with coaches Tim Swartzendruber and women's coach Cy Rolfs of McPherson College. We did not just scrimmage at our camps. All of these coaches and players were actually on the floor running drills and instructing our campers in basketball skills and techniques. Each year, after organizing the camp and contacting the coaches, my job became easy. All I had to do was show up and learn right along with all of the campers.

I remember well one of the biggest compliments I ever received from anyone, while I was coaching basketball. A talented little guard from Piper, Kansas called EJ, who attended our camp all four years of its existence stepped up and said "coach

I've been to six basketball camps this summer, including KU and MU and I just want to let you know that your camp is the best of them all." I thanked him and asked "EJ why do you think that?" He told me you guys all come on the floor with us, and teach us and help us to learn how to improve. At most camps they just divide us into teams and say go play. There is no instruction or help. So that's why I think your camp is the best.

Another coach who graced all four of our camps was Tracey Braden, former women's coach at Westminster College and now head women's basketball coach at the College of the South in Tennessee. Coach Braden is well aware of the events surrounding the Oklahoma State Basketball plane crash and of the history and probable future Pat had in front of him. Coach Braden has said to me: "You can bet that from now on every young lady who

comes into my program from this day forward, will absolutely know the Pat Noyes story." To that I say, Thank you coach Braden!!!

The final two years of the camp the shirts distributed to the participants read: Pat Noyes LWCA Basketball Camp. We promoted the camp as a tribute to Pat.

It is indeed unfortunate we were only able to run this great camp four years, before it was unceremoniously shut down. That's a story in itself, best left for another time

I served as Athletic Director and boys and girls basketball coach for four years. In this time I was also instrumental in hiring a volleyball coach, Dr. Christie Hancock, who played volleyball in college, and started the LWCA volleyball program. Dr. Christie coached the LWCA volleyball team to a winning season, in their first year of competition! We certainly accomplished many good things in just four short years.

During my final two seasons at LWCA we had a tipoff tournament at the school was named for Pat, as the "Pat Noyes Tipoff Tournament." Both years of this tournament we presented a $500 tuition scholarship to an LWCA basketball player, using revenue from the basketball camp to cover the expense. The scholarship was named "The Pat Noyes LWCA Scholarship." Pastor Nick announced the winner of this scholarship, thru tears, both years it was presented.

My tenure at LWCA also came to an unceremonious halt. I just want to note, everything I did and accomplished at LWCA, I did in honor and memory of Pat. Even in death, Pat was continuing to help people through others. By reading this book, it is my hope many more people will also remember Pat in this generous and giving way. It is who and what he truly was. I truly enjoyed my time at LWCA, particularly working with the students. I am convinced I did an amazing job there putting together a successful athletic program for the good of the school and the students. I only regret my time was cut short by some unappreciative people who really did not understand what I had accomplished and how far our program had gone in just four short years. I will always be proud to say I started the athletic program at LWCA, and I did so with Pat in mind.

# Chapter 19: The Aftermath and Other's Lasting Thoughts of Pat

It was now over. A very untimely and unfair ending to Pat's dream, had happened. He and nine other wonderful people were gone forever. The other nine people who perished in the accident on January 27, 2001 are: Daniel Lawson and Nate Fleming, both of whom were OSU basketball players, Will Hancock (sports information employee), Brian Luinstra (trainer), Jared Weiberg (student manager), Kendall Durfey (broadcast engineer), Bill Teegins (KWTV broadcaster), Denver Mills (pilot), and Bjorn Fahlstrom, ( co-pilot). I want to extend my sympathy to each of the families of these nine wonderful men, and ask we all remember them, as we remember Pat. May they all Rest In Peace.

Following are just a few of the many heartfelt comments people have made about Pat, and "the ten" as a group.

Dr. James Halligan, at the time, president of OSU: "They were all wonderful people. We will remember."

Kyle Keller, former OSU assistant coach and now head basketball coach at Stephen F. Austin University: "Those 10 dudes, man, they're the epitome. They were the greatest and happiest people ever. None of them ever had a bad day. We lost the best and happiest guys in our program."

Doug Gottlieb, former Oklahoma State basketball player and ESPN sportscaster, current CBS sports reporter, said the following about Pat in an ESPN magazine article on January 25, 2011.

" Pat Noyes was Oklahoma State Basketball. Pat was little, funny, and full of life. Every recruit we brought in eventually made it to Pat's house where we eventually got them to commit. I remember a recruit calling his brother and telling him that he found a "home" and that he was coming to OSU. Pat made people feel that way. Pat and Sean Sutton were as close as brothers, and I'm not sure Sean ever had the time to truly mourn his friend. And trust me, Pat Noyes was worth mourning."

Derek Joiner, who was Pat's roommate and an OSU student manager for basketball at the time of the plane crash, and Derek is the man who four years after Pat's death married Pat's former girlfriend Stephanie Fisbeck. I would add to this and say I am sure Pat would be happy about the marriage of Stephanie and Derek, as he loved both of them and would want them to have only the best. Again, that was Pat, always looking out for his fellow man. At any rate, here is Derek's touching testimonial to Pat: "I was 20 years old when I first met Pat. I was in Stillwater to work Oklahoma State basketball camp, mainly to impress Pat and the coaches enough to become a student manager. After the week passed, I had no answer. I continued to call Pat for a status update, while working a basketball camp at Tulsa for coach Bill Self. I finally received a message that I would have an opportunity to work at OSU. Pat helped me get setup at OSU with the enrollment people, and he told me which dorm to stay in. When I returned to OSU to begin the semester, I found I was in an older section of the dorm, without airconditioning and was sharing a one person room with another student. Pat came to see me, and he sensed I was uncomfortable with this situation. He walked me 70 feet down the hall to his dorm apartment, with two large bedrooms, a living area and two private bathrooms. He told me I could stay there, until conditions improved in the area of the dorm I was staying in. A week later, he gave me a key to his apartment, and told me I was welcome to stay there. The man ( Pat ) did not know me, but yet showed me his amazing sense of selflessness and humility that it must have taken to allow me to stay there. But that was the way Pat was, doing whatever necessary to help others. I knew he was an astonishing and kind person. He took me to the basketball office and introduced me to everyone, and invited me to social gatherings to meet people, as well. Pat taught me how to tie a neck-tie, and how to hang pants properly, and he even gave me a pair of good dress socks. Over the course of my first semester, Pat helped me in so many ways and with so many things, I can't even begin to remember them all. The apartment Pat allowed me to share is where another friend and myself waited for him to return from Colorado, and sadly he never came back. As time has passed, I have often reflected about Pat and why he was so willing to take me in and help me so much. I think the answer is simple. The day I arrived in Stillwater to work for OSU basketball, I became part of a team. Pat's team, and that was good enough for him. His loyalty to the OSUprogram and to the PEOPLE in that program was second to none. I was now proud to be on PAT'S team. I knew Pat for only five months, yet to this day he stands as one of the most influential people in my life. I think about him when I see his picture in my house, nearly every day. I think about him when I tie a neck-tie, and anytime I go back to Stillwater. I think about Pat when my basketball team falls on hard times, and many times I wear the socks he gave me for big games. I always feel like I owe Pat so much for sharing his knowledge and kindness with me. I continue to try to repay him by sharing the same value of "team", as he did. But believe me, that's one big mortgage to pay!!!"

Derek, I will say this to you, about repaying Pat. You knew him well enough to know he would not want nor expect you or anyone else to pay him back, He would be much happier for you to use the things he taught you to succeed in life. That's who Pat truly was, and what he stood for. Mary and I are extremely proud of the values he lived by, and passed along to others. He was an incredible young man!!!

Coach Eddie Sutton, obviously one of the greatest college basketball coaches of all time with 806 lifetime wins, said simply "Pat had a brilliant basketball mind. If he were to take the toughest test there was concerning basketball knowledge he would score better than 98% of all people taking such a test".This is quite a testimonial from a coach who has won more than 800 games in his coaching career.

Tony Sargent, a good friend of Pat's since he ( Tony ) was 9 or 10 years old, told me about going to basketball camp at Oklahoma State when he was younger. On the last day of camp, the campers were invited to get the autographs of the OSU players who had worked with them at the camp. Tony said he had already gotten most of the autographs he wanted, when he looked and saw Pat standing with a player on the court. Tony approached them and asked "may I have your autograph"? The player told him, "Tony you already got my autograph earlier." To this Tony responded, "I wasn't asking for your autograph, I was asking for Pat's autograph." When Pat told Tony he didn't really think Tony wanted his autograph, Tony responded by saying " I think I really do want your autograph." Laughing, Pat signed Tony's book and said "you better hold on to that. Someday it will be worth a lot of money." Tony said, "I know that, why do you think I wanted it." Tony Sargent was looking to the future he too believed was going to happen for Pat.

And then there is this from Jeff Clark, a teammate of Pat at the Mount, as well as a true friend to Pat and the Noyes family:Pat was the talk of the school from his very first day at the Mount. All the girls thought he was the cutest boy in school. He had a way of making friends with EVERYONE. His assertive personality earned the respect of everyone around him. He was never shy or timid. He left his signature on everything he did, and everyone he came in contact with. He was all heart, and a true friend to all.His passion for sports, his intensity and drive were the fiercest I have ever seen, bar none, by any athlete, amateur or professional. I could not hold my own, with Pat. He always called people by their last name. He was without a doubt, destined to be a great coach, if the lord would have given him more time on this earth. Although Pat was short in stature, he often overshadowed his older brother Dan, who was a real force to be reckoned with himself.

Pat never sacrificed his moral values, although there were plenty of opportunities to do so. He was always in complete control. I used to love staying the night with Pat and Smitty. We had many all nighters talking about girls, hanging at the pool, and playing pick up games in the driveway. He definitely had a home court advantage there and he knew how to use it. He was an absolute genius at overcoming his height disadvantage and knew how to establish position better than most players I've ever seen. I never won a game of 21 against Pat.

He truly made a huge impact on many lives, including mine.

We love and miss you, Patcho,

Clark.

What else can be said about Pat. Jeff Clark really said it all and did the best job he possibly could do, as he told us who Pat was, what his values were, and what all people meant to him, as well as what Pat meant and represented to everyone he knew. As Kyle Keller said about Pat when Kyle was an assistant coach at OSU, with Pat it was "once a friend, always a friend!"

Our heartfelt thanks goes out to Jeff Clark, for his wonderful testimony to Pat. As Pat would have said, thanks, Clark!!!

# Epilogue

This has been the life story of an incredible young man, Patrick Michael Noyes. Everything you have read in this book is true, to the best of my knowledge. It all happened just this way, and basically everything but the ending, is good. For 27 years Pat lived a charmed life and enjoyed every moment, and although the ending is not what we would have liked to have had happen, it is what it is, and nothing can be done to change it. So I have written this book to help preserve his legacy and to convey to all, his lifelong dream to become an NCAA Division 1 Head Basketball coach. Not just a basketball coach, anywhere, but at his alma mater, Oklahoma State University. He was so driven to achieve this goal he would not have been satisfied to coach anywhere else. For Pat it was Oklahoma State, or bust!

The intent of this book is to demonstrate and prove to you, the reader, Pat Noyes was about to make his dream come true and at an extremely young age. He had all the ground work laid, and was waiting for the end of one era at Oklahoma State, which he was positive was about to happen, and then for the "Pat Noyes Era" and dynasty to begin, and last for many years to come. He was going to be the coach that "broke the door in" for the Cowboys, and won multiple national championships.Pat Noyes was well prepared to make this happen. We know he had an extraordinary knowledge of, and love for the game of basketball. He also was a man who related well to every player he came in contact with, and was able to bring the best out of each player he worked with. He did not just develop this relationship with players over night . He had made it his goal to help everyone he ever played the game with, to improve their game to the maximum potential. He began doing this way back when he was playing basketball in the Bradford, Pennsylvania CYO league.

Not only was Pat destined to become a great coach, but he absolutely valued his relationship with every single individual he ever met. There was absolutely nothing he would not do to help anyone in need. He demonstrated this character from the day he was born, until the day his life was tragically ended in a needless plane crash. I was so close to him as he grew up I sometimes could not see or recognize all the good he did for people everywhere. In my research to write this book, I learned many things about Pat his mother nor I ever knew about, until I asked those who knew him to contribute to this effort. Those people could not hold back all the accolades they felt that Pat had earned and deserved.

I also learned, while writing this book everyone grieves such a loss in their own way. No two people do it alike. I often have wondered why since Pat's death has his best friend, his brother Dan, been hesitant to talk with his mom and me about Pat, and why does he not have pictures of Pat displayed throughout his house? As I wrote this book it made me think back, and in doing so I now remember a day in Tyler, Texas several years ago when a lady stepped up to me and said: "Mr. Noyes, Dan was certainly proud of his brother Pat, wasn't he." I asked how she knew this and she told me he talks about Pat all the time, and expresses how much he misses him. Those remarks between Dan's friend and me, finally opened my eyes and made me realize Dan is more comfortable discussing memories of Pat with friends, than he is doing so with relatives. This is his way of grieving, and I never before recognized or took it into consideration. Now the blinders are off, and I do understand, Dan I apologize to you for my lack of understanding your personal grieving process. It won't happen again, and I ask you will please forgive me.

It has been nearly 17 years Pat has been gone, and I have not yet found a way to deal with his loss. I miss him more every day that passes, and in all honesty I don't believe I will ever be at peace again, at least not on this earth. I pray every day for other parents who have lost a child, and I also pray no other parents will ever lose a child, although I realize unfortunately it

will never happen. Parents lose children every day, and I know what those parents are about to begin to endure, and it is a battle no one can win. Mary and I have been to many different grief groups, since we lost Pat, but for the most part it does not help. We need to do our very best to have faith we will see them again, when it's time. I think about the day I will see Pat again, and I have a vision of him meeting me at the gate with a basketball under his arm and saying: "Come on old man, let's go a little one on one." And I'm sure he will "beat me like a drum up there, just like he always did here!!!"

In closing, I ask that we all "Remember The Ten" great men we lost on January 27, 2001. As past OSU President Dr. James Halligan has said, "they were all wonderful people! We will remember." He is absolutely right about this, and they deserve our best efforts to remember each one of them, and to do our best to insure they will never be forgotten. So one more time, "REMEMBER THE TEN," now and forever!!!

This has been the story of Pat Noyes, " The Greatest Coach That Never Was", and very possibly THE GREATEST FRIEND AND HUMANITARIAN THERE EVER WAS!!!

# Acknowledgements

Many people have contributed to and helped me to write this book, and to all of you I want to express my heartfelt thanks! I apologize in advance, to anyone whose name is not included. It is my oversight, should this happen.

Special thanks to Coaches Eddie Sutton and Lefty Driesell, for all you did to make Pat's life everything he wanted it to be.

To Sean Sutton for the special friendship you shared with Pat. Doug Gottlieb said that you were like brothers, and believe me Sean, that meant the world to Pat.

To the students and teachers at Mount Saint Mary High School from 1987-1991. Thank you all for making Pat's high school career and experience so special.

To David Barrett, Michael Schneider, Eric Vogel, coaches Roger Trimmell and Tim Swartzendruber, along with Chad Alexander, thank you all for your creation of the "Pat Noyes Golf Eperience" and scholarship at McPherson College. Also thanks to all who have participated in the golf outing over the past 14 years. Please continue to participate, and recruit your friends to participate as well. It's for an excellent cause, helping provide someone with a scholarship to aid in their pursuit of higher education each year.

Thanks to Mary Lee Gill, Coach Skip Ashworth, Talita Denegri, Doug Kretchmar, Tony Tyler, and the Sisters of Mercy at the Mount. Also special thanks to Mr. Pedro Cordova.

To Matt Mollman, Robert Denegri, Tony and Ty Tyler, who all served so tirelessly to help us and our relatives throughout the entire week at Oklahoma State, thank you so much. We don't know what we would have done without you. Also thanks to Marty Sargent, who over the years since Pat's death has become a very valued friend to us. And to Marty's son

Tony, now an employee of Conference USA, thanks for your testimonial and the drawing of Pat, that we proudly display in our home just above the picture of Pat and President Clinton.

Greg and Elaine Hohensinner, you are the absolute best! Thanks for all you did for us in our time of need, and for all you continue doing for us now. We love you. Also a hearty thank you to Steve and Gena Rieck, Chris and Edie Alford, and Quint and Barb Schillaire all of whom accompanied us from Lansing, Kansas to Stillwater for the traumatic week of Pat's death.

To Jeff Clark, or Clark as Pat would say, we can't thank you enough for your sterling testimonial to Pat. It clearly expresses to all who he was and what he stood for. Thanks, Clark! Also a heartfelt thanks to Layne Jones for sharing his thoughts about Pat.

To Derek and Stephanie Fisbeck Joiner, thanks for your friendship to Pat, and Derek thank you for your kind remembrances of him.

To Dan Searle, a special friend of Pat's from Atlanta Georgia, and Georgia State University, thank you Dan for making the long trip from Atlanta to Stillwater to be with us for the memorial service and Pat's funeral

Thank you Larry Reece, Chris Choat, and Scott Strellar for your participation in the celebration of Pat's life. It was very much appreciated.

Thank you, Dr. James Halligan, for everything you have done and continue to do to make sure "THE TEN" will always be remembered.

Thanks to all who contributed to this book and to all who knew Pat and helped him to lead the very special life that he so much enjoyed and cherished. You are all wonderful people that Mary and I will always remember and hold close to our hearts.

Thanks to Mary's sister Barbara Makarowski and her family and to my brother Glen and his family for coming to be with us from back east, at this trying time in our lives, as well as thanks to Mary's cousins Mary Lou Berner and Linda Berner Al Jundi who also joined us from Memphis, Tennessee.

And finally, we thank our son Dan, and daughter Molly as well as their spouses Robbie and Trevor, and our four wonderful grandchildren Grant, Brady, Lilli, and Owen for all your love and support through this trying time in our lives. We dearly love all of you!!!

CPSIA information can be obtained
at www.ICGtesting.com
Printed in the USA
BVHW071626080719
552849BV00016B/1090/P